Taxcafe Property Guides

How to Profit from Student Property

By Tony Bayliss

Important Legal Notices:

Taxcafe®
PROPERTY GUIDE – "How to Profit from Student Property"

Published by:
Taxcafe UK Limited
214 High St
Kirkcaldy KY1 1JT
United Kingdom
Tel: (01592) 560081

First Edition   November 2006

ISBN 1 904608 48 5

Disclaimer
Before reading or relying on the content of this guide, please read carefully the disclaimer on the last page which applies. If you have queries then please contact the publisher at team@taxcafe.co.uk.

About the Author

Tony Bayliss has been a landlord for over 20 years and his father was a landlord and businessman before him.

Tony trained as a teacher of physical education and drama at Loughborough in the late 1960s, where he obtained a First, and for the following 27 years had an extremely successful career in education, teaching, advising, and inspecting in various parts of England.

In the 1980s, after moving from London to the Midlands, he re-mortgaged his home and bought his first rental property, which he let to students from the local university. Two years later, he bought two more properties and, after ten years, he gave up his full-time job to concentrate on developing his business, going on to create a portfolio of 21 student properties, worth over £4 million.

His teaching background and skill as a communicator made him a natural spokesman for local landlords grappling with emerging legislation, accreditation schemes and other housing initiatives. Amid the frenzied growth of 'buy-to-let', Tony found himself being used increasingly as a consultant to other landlords and as a speaker at training events.

As well as his background in education and property, Tony was a top-class sportsman in his younger days.

He is also an accomplished author, having published poetry in various anthologies, contributed to numerous books, magazines, and Government reports on education, and had two full-length works of fiction published in 2005.

He lists among his interests, world travel, sport, the arts, photographing wildlife, antiques, and DIY.

Dedication

To Jobes, for his support and encouragement.

'Landlord' - An Apology!

The word 'landlord' has unfortunate connotations that don't win us many friends, either from the media, institutions, or legislators.

Few of us own any land to speak of, and even fewer are lords. Many of us are women, yet the alternative title, 'landlady' is just as bad, reminding most people of the anachronistic harridan running a seaside guest house, where hot water for a bath is available only between six and seven on alternate days.

But for want of a better word, I use 'landlord' (and the male pronoun) throughout this book, and I am sorry if it causes offence. It offends me too, but better writers than me have tried and failed to neuter the patriarchal English language.

Landlords are commonly perceived as profiteering from rat-infested slums, or driving up property prices and driving out first-time buyers. Even the financial pages seem to regard us as amateurs, often referring to us collectively as 'Rigbys' or 'Rachmans', suggesting that our way of making a living is somehow unethical.

But most landlords I know aspire to high standards, get on well with their tenants and the community they serve and provide a vital public service. Without landlords, millions would be homeless and our university system would collapse.

This book sets out to support landlords of student properties. It shows how, despite having the odds seemingly stacked against you, it is possible to build a successful business based on high ideals and quality service.

Tony Bayliss

November 2006

Contents

Introduction

I am not an expert on the property market. There is no such animal. Those whom the media put forward as experts have been shown time and time again to be no better than the rest of us at making forecasts.

Take, for example, the legions of experts who lined up in the spring of 2005 and told us unequivocally that a property crash was imminent; and yet they were all wrong. It didn't happen.

But after a brief period of rehabilitation, those same 'experts' will soon be coming out of the woodwork to frighten us with their next piece of fortune-telling, and they may still get it wrong!

The only pattern I have observed time and time again is that when property prices change, they hit London like enormous waves. They have dramatic peaks and troughs, but by the time those waves have reached the Midlands and the north, they are just tiny ripples.

If you want drama, buy property in London. If you want a more peaceful, more predictable life, go to the provinces!

My knowledge of the subject is not based on studying market trends, economic forecasts or consulting tea leaves, but on thirty-five years of buying, renting and selling properties. I am a doer, not just an observer.

As a young teacher in 1971, I scraped together £500 (almost a year's salary!) as a 10% deposit on my first property, a £5,000, two-bedroom flat near the Slough Trading Estate, which was more dreary than even David Brent would have us believe.

But much to my surprise, there followed a property boom and, two years later, I sold the flat for £9,500 and moved to the Midlands. There I bought a proper house for £2,000 less and kept the change to buy furniture and my first colour TV.

And so it went on. I rose quickly to the top rungs of the education career ladder, necessitating several moves to different parts of the country in the process.

Because my growing family needed ever larger houses, I always stretched myself to the limit in buying the biggest and best property I could afford. This included two moves to London, labouring under the burden of very painful mortgages.

But after 15 years I owned outright the house I lived in and ten years after that, when I had left my full-time job, I suddenly realised that my home was worth more than all the money I had earned throughout my entire career in education.

So it was my own experience, not the tips and forecasts of experts, that showed me that the £500 I had first invested had grown to over £300,000 in just over twenty five years, an increase of nearly 60,000%!

Did you get that? SIXTY THOUSAND PERCENT!

It was this realisation that persuaded me to chuck in the full-time job and turn my hobby into my second career. In any case, the prospect of surviving one day on a meagre teacher's pension was not one I could get very excited about.

From Home Owner to Landlord

My interest in letting had been instilled in me since childhood. My father had managed to buy an enormous old house in the early 1950s and had converted parts of it into flats for families from the local air force base. They had their own entrance so we shared no communal areas but I have fond memories of always having people around, especially other children.

So, to supplement my own family income there had often been lodgers in my own house too, and my children loved it just as I had done.

But it wasn't until I moved away from the south-east for a second time in the mid-Eighties, exchanging a fairly substantial semi in Harrow for a cheaper nine-bedroom mansion in the Midlands, that we got into lodgers in a big way.

The local university was frantically advertising for rooms, claiming that vast numbers of students faced the prospect of sleeping on floors for want of local lodgings.

So I offered a rather pokey attic bedroom that my family didn't use, and had nearly a hundred phone calls within a week of it being advertised.

I suddenly realised there was money to be made here, and the seeds of my new business were sown!

For the following four years there was a succession of student lodgers, but I eventually summoned up the courage to buy my first student house in 1991 by re-mortgaging my own home.

In those days, buy-to-let mortgages didn't exist and re-mortgages had to be for a specific 'approved' purpose. But given that I owned the house outright, there was plenty of equity available for the loan, and I took three further extensions to that loan over the next few years.

In the early Nineties, property prices were low and going nowhere. London was still recovering from a crash in the late Eighties, and with thousands of people in negative equity, there were lots of repossessed properties being pushed on to the market by the lenders. So bargains were easy to find, even though prospects for capital growth seemed gloomy.

But I wasn't thinking about capital growth at the time. All I cared about was getting the new house tenanted to cover my monthly mortgage repayments and other costs, and to make a little profit each month.

In the event, some student friends of one of my lodgers came to view the house even before I had exchanged sale contracts and they signed tenancy agreements on the spot. That pattern was to repeat itself many times in the years to come.

The value of that first house didn't increase at all for six years. But after fourteen years I sold it for four-and-a-half times the purchase price. I had made a healthy profit each year from rental income too, with rents rising and mortgage repayments dropping as interest rates went down.

Such was the demand from students for good quality accommodation that I bought two more properties in 1993 and another two in 1995, all by re-mortgaging my home.

Buy-to-Let Mortgages

By the late Nineties, buy-to-let mortgages arrived and with them, a discernible change of attitude among the lenders.

Previously, a loan on a property that wasn't your own home meant signing away your life with extra cover, being forced to take out the ill-fated endowment mortgages, finding guarantors, or promising that you changed your underwear at least once a week.

When buy-to-let mortgages arrived, the lenders were falling over themselves to give away money without any reference to your income, age, sex or any of the myriad checks they had insisted upon previously.

Now, almost anyone can borrow money to buy a house to let, just so long as it values up to the purchase price and has the potential to earn more rent than the monthly loan repayments.

Unlike some investors, however, I didn't throw caution to the wind when buy-to-let mortgages arrived and go for massive expansion. I moved along slowly, choosing properties that were in the right area and of the right type, making sure there was still an on-going demand from students for what I was offering.

And because I was now doing this full time and being on the wrong side of fifty, there was a limit to what I wanted to take on.

By 2004 I had 21 properties and decided that was enough. Others, younger and more ambitious and maybe more reckless, would have gone on playing re-mortgage leapfrog, and good luck to them, but that wasn't what I wanted.

The fundamental difference in what I did compared with most landlords with a reasonably-sized portfolio, was to continue to manage it all myself, and that is what a lot of this book is about.

Chapter 1

The Buy to Let Property Market

Following the slump in the property market in the late Eighties, which by no means affected every type of property or every geographical area, investors saw the Nineties as a good time to buy.

I would argue that, provided you are sure of your rental market and choose the right kind of property in the right location, it is always a good time to buy.

Nevertheless, I managed to find some real bargains back in those heady days. I was buying properties for £30,000-£40,000, spending £10,000 on refurbishment, and taking gross annual rents that were around 15% of my outlay.

At the time of writing this book, rental yields of 5-8% are more the norm. But that doesn't take account of capital growth of course which, provided you hold on to the property long enough, has shown consistently since the Second World War that property is one of the best places to put your money.

In the 20 years that I have been buying and selling rental houses, my average annual gain in capital value has been 12% (based on actual selling prices). This was despite frequently breaking the golden rule of not selling within three years and thus not getting any capital gains tax taper relief.

So even given today's low rental returns, my experience is that, taking rent and capital growth together, the buy-to-let investor can reckon on an overall minimum return of around 17% a year. As rents start to climb, that figure can easily exceed 20%. During boom times it can even approach three figures.

The arrival of buy-to-let mortgages in the late Nineties saw a massive growth in the number of landlords, many owning only one or two rental properties, who cashed in on the property price boom that occurred between 2000 and 2004.

In London, the number of registered landlords offering student properties doubled in that period. This figure didn't take account of the large numbers of parents who bought a house for their children to live in while at university.

But when the doom merchants started talking up a property price crash in 2004 there was a mass exodus, the number of registered London landlords dropping back by 25%. This pattern appears to have been replicated in many other parts of the country.

New Regulations

Another factor contributing to this exodus was the proposed housing legislation, which talked about a national licensing scheme and hung over landlords like the Sword of Damocles for nearly three years.

Thanks to pressure put on ministers by The Residential Landlords Association and other lobbyists, the proposals were eventually watered down to something more reasonable and manageable.

But when it became clear in early 2004 that properties with three or more storeys and five or more unrelated tenants would fall under the licensing scheme, many landlords, including myself, dropped this type of property from their portfolios.

Obviously some landlords were simply not prepared to upgrade their properties to meet the new standards. But even those landlords who could comply decided to sell because of the on-going cost of licensing, the form filling and the extra rounds of inspections.

It was simply more hassle than it was worth. I happen to know that only one of the people who bought one of the larger properties I sold has bothered to apply for a licence and non-compliance with the licensing scheme is already becoming a problem.

But why bother buying these very large houses anyway? Students have changed a lot over the years, and their needs and requirements now drive the market. Most don't like living in very big groups.

I used to have houses offering six, seven, eight, and even one with nine bedrooms, which had been a former nursing home. But they became less popular and now most students seem to want to be in groups of no more than five, with properties for two to four being the most popular.

Obviously this has implications for the rent you can charge, because the overheads on a small house are pretty much the same as on a large one. But despite what you may read about students being poor, there will always be those who will pay for the right property.

Local Councils have the authority to extend the licensing scheme, and while at present it is restricted to three-storey properties with five or more tenants, in areas where there is a glut of student housing, local authorities may feel justified in extending it to include all student properties.

I am sure this will happen in some areas and it pays to be ready for this. It's easier and cheaper to refurbish a property to the right standards when it is unoccupied than to do first-aid work when it's let or furnished.

So check on standards required by the licensing scheme and in the local accreditation scheme and try to meet them from the outset. Not only will your tenants be safer. It will make your property more marketable.

Tony's Tips

- There is never a bad time to buy property.

- Ignore the 'experts' predictions about price rises and falls – they are more often wrong.

- Anticipate an extension to the licensing scheme by refurbishing your student property to the highest possible safety standards.

Chapter 2

Why Students?

'Students are noisy and upset the neighbours, don't pay their rent, mess up the properties, and only stay for half the year' – right?'

Wrong.

Students are the future teachers, industrialists, scientists, doctors, lawyers, dotcom entrepreneurs and other highly skilled professionals who hold the future of our country in their hands.

But they all suffer from one condition that makes some landlords wary of them: they are young.

In my experience, 99% of students are reasonable, intelligent, polite, and just want secure, clean, good-quality accommodation so that they can get on with their studies.

If they are treated with courtesy and consideration and given a good level of service, they rarely cause problems. Let's look at that list of stereotypes again:

'Students are noisy and upset the neighbours'

I got into the habit of logging complaints some years ago so that, should there be any comeback about my not taking appropriate action, I would be able to quote dates and times in my defence.

Looking at my log, I see the number of complaints about my tenants from neighbours is eleven in fifteen years.

However, the number of complaints by my tenants about their neighbours is twenty-nine. So it seems to me that students are less noisy than most families and they really need some peace and quiet to get on with their work.

Of course these complaints are not my responsibility but both tenants and neighbours appreciate it if I act as mediator. It certainly helps to secure good relationships when I do so.

If the matter cannot be resolved amicably, the complainant needs to refer the matter to the local council but, as the law stands, the landlord is not responsible.

Example

One of the most difficult incidents I had to deal with was a complaint by two female tenants. It was about the other two they had chosen to live with, having come to me as a group of four friends.

Fireworks were flying and I tried to reason with both sides, even offering my daughter – a trained counsellor – as a mediator.

I always try to help in these situations but the intervention of a landlord can often make things worse. Two of them demanded that I provide alternative accommodation. I had no obligation to do this but, as luck would have it, I did have two vacant rooms in a nearby house.

But they turned up their noses, saying the rooms weren't as nice. This led me to believe the situation wasn't as bad as they claimed, so I left them to it.

A week later I went off to Australia for ten days to watch England win the Rugby World Cup and, on my return, found that two of the girls had done a runner. At that time of year I was unable to re-let their rooms so I started writing to their parents, who had signed guarantees, asking for rent.

The parents ignored my letters and so, eventually, I had to launch a claim against them in the County Court for non-payment of rent.

The parents' defence against my claim hinged on the assertion that, by not sorting out the squabble, I had not shown their daughter proper 'duty of care' and they were justified in walking away from the contract, and not paying the rent.

The parents' resolve to resist my claim was bolstered by a letter of support they received from the Students' Union, which misguidedly agreed that I had been in breach of contract.

In court, the judge patiently explained to the parents that I had gone far beyond my legal and contractual obligations and that it wasn't my job to sort out their daughters' squabbles. That, he said, was a job for parents to address.

Case won, parents with tails between their legs, students' union red-faced.

But let me emphasise that this experience was a rarity, and is the only time I have had to take a tenant or guarantor to a court hearing. All other disputes, and they have been very rare, have been settled out of court.

'Students don't pay their rent'

When I was a student in the Sixties, higher education was free. Well, not quite. For those from middle- to low-income families, tuition, board, and lodging were free, and there was a grant to cover books, equipment... and beer.

Wealthier parents had to pay for board and lodging and were supposed to give their children the equivalent of the grant but tuition was still free. We didn't feel rich but compared with today's students we lived in halcyon days.

Actually, my father earned too much for me to get a grant and refused to give me money. He believed higher education was a waste of time, so I worked twelve hours a day for a building firm during every vacation to save enough to get me through (and learned a lot of DIY skills in the process!).

I was able to survive quite comfortably but that experience enables me to empathise closely with the plight of today's students.

Student Loans and Tuition Fees

In the Nineties, grants were abolished and replaced with student loans, encouraging the idea that it's now OK in this country to go through life in debt, never mind the social and personal consequences.

And just at the time when the camel's back of student finance was groaning under growing bales of debt, the student-friendly socialist government decided it was a good time to make students pay for their tuition too, presumably diverting the money saved to fight the war in Iraq.

Students have now come to accept that they will graduate with debts of £20,000 or £30,000 and, frankly, I have nothing but admiration for the way most of them cope with this horrendous imposition. A few don't, of course.

And yet, despite their worsening financial position, students do pay their rent. My rent collection record was virtually 100% until three or four years ago, and has never dropped below 99%.

'Listening Landlord'

But the key to this high collection record is not just to sit back and expect the rent to roll in on time, because it won't.

You have to be persistent but flexible, recognising that student finance is usually based on their receiving loan payments in October, January and April. This means it's best to agree a contract that asks for payments at those times if they prefer it that way.

Sometimes loans arrive late because of the bureaucratic minefield students have to negotiate in securing their finance. I always agree to accept backdated cheques or delays in payment, provided the student talks to me and tells me what is going on.

Those who bury their heads in the sand and prefer to forget they owe rent are told there will be penalties for late payment. This is usually deducted from the deposit at the end of the tenancy.

So by adopting the stance of a 'listening landlord' and using a careful balance of stick and carrot underpinned by an insistence that all students have a UK-based rent guarantor, most rent is collected without fuss.

Only on very rare occasions is it necessary to rattle bars with letters that talk about the last resort being court action.

'Students mess up the properties'

It's certainly true that without a parent there to nag about the condition of a bedroom, most students enjoy living in total squalor, but that's their choice, provided it's safe squalor. It really is the exceptional student who cleans more than once a year, who changes bed linen or who notices that the entire bedroom floor is covered in debris.

But when it comes to communal areas, most disputes in shared houses arise because some people make the mess and other people are expected to clear it up.

As a landlord, I suggest that they agree and adhere to a cleaning rota, but few actually seem to achieve this. I only intervene when, on visiting a property for another purpose, find communal areas so cluttered and untidy that they are actually dangerous.

I write a polite letter pointing this out and giving a date and time when I will return for a 'health and safety' inspection. It always works.

This device is particularly useful when I want to show people around who are looking for rooms for the following year. Surprisingly, prospective tenants are often put off by a dirty house even though they will probably end up making it more dirty themselves!

I gave up long ago trying to forecast which group of new tenants would be most untidy. All the stereotypes about first impressions are ill founded.

First Impressions (Don't) Count

For example, I've had groups of well-groomed, Home County girls who, when viewing the property were immaculately dressed and sweet-smelling. They walked around with clipboards containing parent-inspired check-lists, examining everything before finally taking the property with winning smiles and polite handshakes.

These types were bound to be perfect tenants, I usually thought.

But within a few weeks of moving in, they were often behind with rent, had piled empty rotting boxes outside the front of the house, couldn't work the vacuum cleaner or change the proverbial light bulb. They had painted the walls purple and, frankly, hadn't got a clue about independent living.

Then at the other extreme, I've had all-male groups who were threateningly large and scruffy, wore hoodies and walked around during the viewing emitting uncommunicative grunts. They kicked at doors and enjoyed private jokes, which I was sure were about me, but later turned out to be model tenants in every way.

In fact the tidiest tenants I ever had were just such an all-male group, one of whom appointed himself as the 'sergeant-major' and posted large notices all around the house telling the others to "Clean the !*#£%?@ Bath After Use or Else", etc.

The other tenants seemed to love it – they stayed for three years, all paid their rent in full and on the button, and still send me Christmas cards.

But despite the mess in most student houses, it is all very superficial, and they rarely do any real damage to the properties.

Normal Wear and Tear

Like most landlords, I have a clause in my tenancy agreement saying that the property must be returned to me in the same condition as when the tenants moved in, 'normal wear and tear accepted', and that there will be deductions from deposits if this doesn't happen.

In reality, even those who clean up really well and get their deposits back, never do so to my standards.

I always like to hand over a property that I feel is clean enough for me or a member of my family to live in, so I routinely send in professional cleaners after the tenants have left.

When the cleaners have finished, I do all the minor repairs to furniture and furnishings, and paint out marks on walls.

Even after the dirtiest property is handed back it is possible to have it ready for new tenants within two days.

'Students only stay for half the year'

The standard university year is 36-40 weeks and I always operate on the basis that my tenants come in late September and stay for 40 weeks, paying a retainer for the summer period. The retainer I charge is about 25% of the rent.

But there are now so many different types and lengths of courses, with different start and end points, that is it impossible for the landlord to standardise a tenancy period that will suit all students.

Moreover, an increasing number of students, whose universities are in city areas but whose homes are more rural, prefer to stay in their student properties for the full twelve months, knowing they can get work in the university town during the vacation periods.

I was really quite happy with a forty-week tenancy and a summer retainer because it meant I could get good access to properties between tenancies to do proper cleaning and maintenance when they were unoccupied.

In any case, students were paying me a higher rent in 40 weeks than I could get from a family in 52 weeks.

A family would regard a house with three rooms upstairs and two downstairs as suitable for perhaps two parents and two children.

When letting the same house to students, one of the downstairs rooms counts as a fourth bedroom. Provided the property is well furnished and complies with all the safety requirements, the rent charged can easily be twice the amount charged to the family because it is calculated on the basis of rent per room per week.

Of course, some students have got wise to this and now go to commercial letting agents where they can find these cheaper family houses.

However, they usually need furnishing, are in less favourable locations and rarely have the usual safety features found in student houses.

But an increasing number of landlords are not content with forty-week tenancies and now demand a full fifty-two-week commitment.

Last year, this was the case with 55% of all registered landlords in London. Where students don't ask for this, but landlords demand it, I think this greediness brings shame on us all. It doesn't help to dispel the stereotype of the profiteering, unfeeling landlord.

If profit is your only aim, then this might be for you but personally, unless students actually want a 52 week tenancy, I would never insist upon it.

In the same way that we expect tenants to understand that we cannot afford to have empty rooms not earning money, and so charge summer retainers, I think we should be more understanding about their perilous financial situation.

We should not expect them to pay full rent throughout the whole summer when they have no need to use the property and when we are probably using their absence to do our annual maintenance anyway.

How to Stave off the Competition

Given that the university year is only about 38 weeks, a minimum tenancy period of 40, or even 44 weeks, seems to be a more reasonable compromise for both parties.

Landlords should perhaps ask themselves whether they would be happy for their own cash-strapped sons and daughters to hand over half their summer earnings to a landlord for rooms they are not using.

In any case, if you are operating in a highly competitive area where there are more rooms than students, you will fall victim to market forces if potential tenants have the choice between your 52 weeks and your rival's 44. The net difference in income achieved is hardly worth the hassle.

Tony's Tips

- Treat students well, and they will always be good tenants.

- With firm but friendly persistence, rent collection rates from students can be virtually 100%.

- When faced with charges against their deposits, students almost always hand the property back in good condition.

- Ask for a minimum tenancy of 40-44 weeks, with a summer retainer. If you demand a 52-week tenancy from students who don't want it, they will go to your rivals.

Chapter 3

The Student Rental Market

Expansion, Expansion, Expansion!

Be in no doubt that the student rental market is here to stay, is expanding, and has been doing so for the last 50 years.

Successive post-war governments have all put an expansion of higher education near the top of their manifestos. Even though the rhetoric hasn't always matched the reality, the growth in the number of university places in recent decades has been nothing short of phenomenal.

In 1959 only 4% of 18 to 21-year-olds were at university, but by 1989 that figure had grown to 18%. Universities were no longer able or willing to provide campus accommodation for all students, and so the private sector stepped in.

By 2006, the figure attending university had climbed to 43%, still well short of the Government's much-publicised target of 50%. Even that may yet be increased given that the percentage attending in parts of the US and some European countries is already in the region of 60%. So there is a strong imperative for politicians to continue the trend.

Rightly or wrongly, they equate the future wealth and prosperity of the country with the numbers of students going to university.

Hence Tony Blair's mantra "Education, education, education" (those of us in property know that what he actually said was "Regulation, regulation, regulation"!).

But more students are obviously good news for landlords. So long as there remains a strong political will from all sides of the House to increase the number of full-time places in higher education, there will be more and more students needing accommodation.

Living Away from Home

When grants were abolished a few years ago, we all thought the numbers of students needing rented rooms would fall because many would choose to apply to their local university and take the cheaper option by living at home.

This supposition ignored two overriding factors. Firstly, students want to go to the best possible university to suit their study needs – which is rarely their local establishment.

But more importantly, for most students, university is a rite of passage. It involves being away from home for the first time, meeting new friends and doing all those things that make student life a unique and necessary experience before the reality of a nine-to-five job.

It is extremely difficult, if not impossible, for these experiences to be had while living under the parental roof. Moreover, despite the tears on waving their darlings goodbye, most parents are really quite pleased to have the house to themselves again.

With the introduction of higher tuition fees in the autumn of 2006, many universities reported a drop in applications. Figures are still up on three years ago, so I fully expect this to be a minor adjustment and once people are used to the idea of paying tuition fees, numbers will restart their inexorable climb.

Halls of Residence

Even though education is a government priority, most 'new' money goes into schools rather than universities.

It is rumoured that the idea of introducing tuition fees came not from politicians or civil servants but from university vice-chancellors, who were finding it difficult to make ends meet.

Many of us think it regrettable that we are now nearer to the American model of funding for universities than the model in many European countries, where higher education is state funded and still largely free to the student.

But the reality is that government funding of higher education in the UK simply has not kept pace with its expansion.

When this happens, the first things to go are the frills, and this includes halls of residence.

Most universities provide only sufficient rooms in halls of residence for a limited number and these places are usually prioritised for first-year students. This means the others have to find accommodation in the local community.

Moreover, the rents charged for rooms in the halls of residence, which are usually only squalid single bedrooms off dark corridors, are often a third higher than rooms in shared houses.

The consequence is that once students have arrived and found new friends in their first year, they can't wait to get out of hall and find a house. The universities encourage this by acting as letting agents for private landlords.

Almost all have accommodation units that advertise private properties. Many, in conjunction with their local councils, now have accreditation schemes that encourage landlords to meet standards that are usually a lot higher than those achieved in the halls of residence.

More on accreditation schemes later.

Overseas Students

Whatever we may think of the current standards in our education system, the view persists in many parts of the world that British is best.

Parents from overseas are queuing up to send their children to British schools and universities. This is despite the fact that tuition fees for overseas students are up to three times higher than for home students and annual living and travelling expenses may exceed what an average worker back in their own country could earn in a lifetime.

Overseas students are, therefore, a lucrative source of income for our universities. Many are milking this by setting up twinning arrangements with other universities abroad or establishing satellites in far-flung places with the aim of encouraging more students from abroad to study in the UK.

In London, the number of overseas students in higher education in 2004-2005 was 22%, and this figure is matched, and often exceeded, in other metropolitan areas up and down the UK.

The majority of these students have already done a first degree in their own country, and come to the UK to do post-graduate studies usually lasting only one or maybe two years.

Very few are offered places in halls of residence and their late arrival often means there is a last-minute scramble to find them somewhere to live. Most team up with other expats, and hire a private house or flat.

Tony's Tips

- Student numbers are growing every year, so there is an on-going need for more private accommodation.

- Students prefer sharing houses or flats to living in halls of residence.

- Universities increasingly depend on the private sector to house their students.

- The number of students from abroad is increasing.

Chapter 4

Choosing Your Location

Live Locally

If you are just starting out with your first student property my best advice is to make sure you are living near a university, and buy something local that you can manage easily.

It is likely that you have borrowed a large sum of money to buy the property. The difference between the mortgage repayments, the insurance, other basic costs and the rent received, doesn't leave you with sufficient margin to give away a further 10-15% to a letting agent simply because you live too far away.

Organising the property maintenance from a distance is also very costly. The agent will call in expensive contractors to do even the smallest of jobs and will rarely give your property the tender loving care it deserves.

Indeed, you may wonder just what you are getting from the agent for your money. The reason is that most agents are only really interested in setting up tenancies and not in the day-to-day minutiae of managing the properties. They rarely leave their desks, so they could be just as far away as you are for all the difference they make.

By living locally, you can do most of the little jobs yourself, no matter how inexpert you think you are at DIY.

Once your property is bought, refurbished to the right standards and furnished, the only contractors you really need are specialists to service gas and electrical installations.

Why pay call-out charges and exorbitant hourly rates for people to unblock vacuum cleaners, change a mattress or replace a broken hinge when you can do these little tasks yourself, and thus preserve your profit?

But as your portfolio grows, and you build up a team of trusted contractors, there is less reason for you to be on hand, because economies of scale kick in and you will get discounts (and better service) from contractors who look after your whole portfolio. And they like the steady work!

At that stage you are better able to manage everything by mobile phone or email. Most of the 'bigger' landlords I know started off with a few properties close to their homes. Once the size of the portfolio reached double figures, they were able to move on to a different location, with the reassurance that their team of regular contractors could cover all eventualities in their absence.

For the past six years I have split my week between two different parts of the country and taken frequent prolonged holidays abroad.

My tenants have the phone numbers of people to contact if they can't reach me. Such is my confidence in my various contractors, I can always be sure on my return that problems and maintenance issues have been dealt with quickly and efficiently. Subsequent invoices are always fairly based on work genuinely done. Any contractor not responding promptly, or over-charging is taken off the list.

Check Out Your Local University

It never ceases to amaze me that people go into business without doing any market research or having any special knowledge of their field.

My father was a carpenter who restored old caravans and then went on to make vast sums of money in the caravan trade. He knew, loved, and understood caravans.

Just after the war, people needed somewhere to live and caravans (now called 'mobile homes'!) were a cheap alternative to houses. There was a ready market, and my father did well.

But when he sold up and retired, a drinking buddy persuaded him to invest the larger portion of his wealth in a diamond mine. He trusted his friend, but knew nothing about diamonds, and lost the lot.

A Lucrative Market – If You Do Your Research

When I was selling some properties recently on a landlords' website, I was inundated with enquiries from prospective buyers, ranging from established landlords through to those who didn't even own their own home, and were tenants themselves.

They all had two things in common. They knew absolutely nothing about the student market but they had been told it was very lucrative.

They thought that if they bought up-and-running student houses in a student city they could just sit back puffing their cigars at the other end of the country and watch the money roll in to their bank accounts.

Sorry guys, it just ain't that simple.

The first thing you need to do is make sure there will be a constant flow of prospective tenants. The best way to do this is to go to the accommodation unit at your local university.

Perhaps, in the first instance, you could phone pretending to be a parent or student, and ask for accommodation lists to be sent to you. This will give you an idea of the type, range, and location of the properties available, and also what rents are being charged.

Bear in mind that this may only show properties currently available and that there may be many more already let.

Next, get a good map and walk the streets around the university sites to get a feel for the area, noting in particular the streets where most of the properties on your list are situated.

Ask yourself why some streets have lots of rental houses and others seem to have none.

On your travels, you will see notices in windows offering rooms to students. Make appointments to see some of them.

How long have they been empty? If you get the impression that they are hard to let, ask yourself why that might be.

Are they clean and well furnished and do they have all the usual safety features? Are they too far from the university? Is the street run-down and generally unappealing or even dangerous, and so on.

Next, go to the accommodation unit as a prospective landlord and ask whether they think there is a demand for student properties in the area.

They may thrust details of their accreditation scheme in your face and explain that your property needs to be inspected before they will advertise it. But ask what percentage of landlords actually use their system (they may not know, or may lie!) as opposed to putting up posters in windows.

Ask about recruitment to the university and whether there are plans to expand numbers, to build new halls of residence (which would compete with you), to open new university sites, or to close old ones.

I know a landlord who mortgaged himself to the hilt buying three properties close to a university site only to find that the site was being closed the following year and the students relocated to another location four miles away. He sold at a massive loss.

From the Horse's Mouth

Of course, the best people to ask are the students themselves. You could position yourself outside the Students' Union building or go into the bar and do your own vox pop.

Ask students about the best and worst places to live, what rent they pay or would be willing to pay, whether it's difficult to find accommodation, and so on.

This will probably be the best and most reliable source of information, because these are the clients, the people who sign contracts. Their views are the ones that count.

The point of all these enquiries is to arm you with enough information to decide whether there will be a sufficient demand from students for the property you intend to buy.

It will give you a good idea whether the rents you are likely to achieve will make the whole exercise worthwhile.

Survey of University Towns

Even though your search will focus on a particular locality, there are some national trends worth bearing in mind.

My own family have attended universities in Loughborough, London, Leeds, Birmingham, St Albans, Bristol and Oxford. The main difference between those places is the price of buying a property.

The enquiries you make will contain the same elements wherever you are but clearly some areas may already be more saturated with student properties than others. But don't let that put you off.

In preparation for writing this book, I conducted a survey, sending out questionnaires to all UK university accommodation units. It aimed to find out which areas are 'hot' and which are still 'cool' for the investor.

The overwhelming conclusion was that there was still a demand for quality student accommodation in almost every urban area serving a university.

Numbers of students are still rising, universities are **not** prioritising the building of new halls of residence and the introduction of licensing and accreditation schemes is discouraging landlords who provide sub-standard accommodation.

Very few areas reported a saturation of student houses, and even here there was still scope for landlords aspiring to higher standards.

Loughborough
Loughborough told me there were more houses than students because a lot of new building had taken place. But here the recently introduced accreditation scheme had yet to bite into black-market accommodation and enforcement of the licensing scheme was driving some landlords out of business.

Here, as in many other places, the market was reported as being 'student led'. This means that if you give students what they really want, then even in Loughborough there are still opportunities for investors.

Loughborough has 5,000 students wanting private accommodation, so anyone offering quality is bound to find a market.

London
In London there are roughly 250,000 students requiring private housing. Westminster University alone has 25,000 students but provides hall accommodation for only 1,500.

Over half of all London students sign full 12-month tenancy agreements and rents range from £90-120 per week per room.

Of course the problem with London, as with places like Oxford and Bristol, is the cost of buying the property in the first place. Also, the rental yields (rent expressed as a percentage of purchase price) are lower than in places like **Nottingham**, **Walsall** or **Leeds**.

But in the more expensive cities, the capital growth is likely to be higher.

For the cost of a two-bedroom flat in a poorer area of London you can buy a substantial house in almost any city area north of Milton Keynes.

It doesn't take a genius to work out that the return from five or six tenants in a big house is always going to be higher than two students in a London flat, even though rents in London may be twice as high as in the Midlands and the north.

York
Let's look at York as an example. For the same price as our small flat in London, we can buy a substantial house only a mile from the centre of York.

I am looking at a house on a website that has four double bedrooms and two reception rooms, one of which will act as the fifth bedroom. The house is priced at £180,000, has an upstairs bathroom and second toilet downstairs, which will make the house very attractive to students.

The Accommodation Officer at the University of York reports that in the current year 5,600 students need private accommodation but that there is currently only capacity in the private sector for 3,500-4,000, meaning that around 2,000 additional rooms in private houses are needed – that's about 400 houses!

The rent the students in York pay for a room in the university halls of residence ranges from £67.06 to £81.41 per week, whereas the typical rent in a student house is currently £55 per room per week.

So, assuming that you pay £180,000 for a five-bed house in York (and there are many cheaper than that) and rent it out for the full year at £55 per student per week, your revenue return will be nearly 8% a year.

It will be even higher if you go for a six-bedroom house (and don't forget to add to that any gain in the property value). York is very typical of most Midlands and northern cities where there are still rich pickings for landlords of student properties.

Here are some other examples of the current scene:

Oxford
New halls of residence have recently been completed in the city centre but there is still a massive need for private accommodation, most of which is situated in the northern suburbs.

House prices are high – a house with capacity for five bedrooms will set you back at least £250,000-300,000. But rents are also high, with students willing to pay £75-100 a week each, so your return will be in the range of 7-9%.

Birmingham
As with most universities, only about a third of students are given rooms in hall. The remainder (20,000 of them!) have to find somewhere in the local community.

Property in the Edgbaston area is expensive and hard to find. However, if you go in the other direction towards Selly Oak and Bournbrook you can pick up a large house for well under

£200,000. Rents are £55-60 per student per week so your return is comparable to that in York.

Cardiff

Cardiff, like Loughborough, claims there are more houses than students. But given that it doesn't have an accreditation scheme involving inspections, it would appear there is still a proliferation of sub-standard housing. Students will almost certainly respond well to entrepreneurial landlords offering quality accommodation.

The ratio between property prices and rents in Cardiff is similar to those in York and Birmingham.

Belfast

Belfast has lots of low-quality student accommodation, some as cheap as £25 per room per week, but the manager of the university accommodation unit tells me that there is a dire shortage of better accommodation.

The University of Ulster adopts a hands-off approach to landlords, having no accreditation scheme and not even asking for safety certificates before it will advertise private accommodation to its students.

There are plenty of four-bedroom, two-reception-room houses for sale in Belfast for under £150,000. With rents at the top end reaching £80, there is potential to achieve returns of well over 10%.

So Belfast is definitely a hot spot at the moment, and with the university treating everyone like grown-ups by not demanding a paper-chase before they advertise your property, there are fewer hurdles to clamber over than elsewhere.

Wolverhampton

Wolverhampton is at the opposite end of the spectrum in terms of paper chasing, having introduced a rigorous inspection-based accreditation scheme many years ago. It resulted in a big sell-up by some landlords and a further sell-up of three-storey properties when licensing was first mooted.

Standards of accommodation have, therefore, risen but less than half of private landlords choose to be accredited.

Landlords of the 'better' properties report that they are always tenanted and many are expanding their portfolios, buying up from those unable to cope with the competition.

A large house in the two main student areas of the city, Penn Fields and Whitmore Reans, costs around £150,000. Rents are about £50 per tenant per week and rising, giving a potential return of over 8% per annum.

Edinburgh

Edinburgh reports that they are 'desperate' for more private accommodation, with 13,000+ students on roll, only a third of whom find a place in halls of residence.

As in other areas, many owners of substandard accommodation have sold up, unable to finance improvements to meet the standards of the accreditation scheme that is operated by the local council, and involves inspections.

There is particular need for flats and apartments close to the university, but also for larger houses further out.

Other Places?

Do your own research by calling the accommodation unit at your local university (they all have websites with contact details), asking if they are short of quality accommodation.

Enquire whether they have an accreditation scheme, what average rents are, and then check the local estate agents' websites to see whether suitable properties are available and affordable.

Overseas Students

Most of the universities in urban areas report a significant number of students from overseas.

For example, Loughborough has 14%, Belfast 20%, London 22%, Wolverhampton 27%, Edinburgh, Cardiff and Oxford have around 30%. These figures are said to be increasing, especially with the expansion of the European Union.

While this might appear to be good news for the landlord, the problem with overseas students is they rarely have UK-based guarantors. Landlords are being asked to take them on without any assurance that they will pay their rent. UK civil courts have no jurisdiction abroad, so launching a claim for unpaid rent is pointless.

Example

A friend of mine recently filled a house with Nigerian post-graduate students, over in the UK for one year. These students seemed to be excellent tenants in every way. They looked after the house well, were always polite and charming, and always paid their rent on time... until the last few months, when they all simply stopped paying.

My friend despaired. The tenants smiled sweetly, but refused to pay, and it's difficult to punch a smiling face!

There was no point in evicting them because the procedure would be costly. Given the time-scale involved it would also be futile, and he did not know where to turn for help.

He asked the Students' Union but they weren't interested and told him it was a private matter for him to sort out himself.

At the end of the tenancy, the students left, all owing nearly three months' rent, and went home to Nigeria.

My friend made a substantial loss on that property and vowed he would never take overseas students again.

Given that universities are going out of their way to attract students from overseas because of the higher tuition fees collected, it seems to me they should face up to their responsibilities here. They should give local landlords some help by guaranteeing student rents instead of just dumping these students on the local community.

Most universities already have provisions in place for withholding academic awards from students who leave university owing money for tuition fees and books. However, they claim they cannot extend this to private-sector rents for contractual reasons.

Not true, because in London, the threat of a boycott of overseas students by landlords produced a scheme now adopted by many of the city's universities in which they guarantee rents for all properties that are fully accredited.

In other words, the accommodation is contracted by the university, so tenants who do not pay their rent face sanctions by the university rather than by the landlord.

Sooner or later, provincial universities will have to follow suit if they are to avoid an accommodation crisis by landlords refusing to take on overseas students without UK guarantees.

Choosing the Right Area and Street

I wish I'd had a book like this to help me when I first started out, because I made some dreadful mistakes!

In the early Nineties, prices were at a standstill and so there was very little property on the market.

Interest rates were in double figures and people were just gritting their teeth and staying at home. But having already bought two houses, both of which were tenanted and doing well, I was keen to expand.

One day I saw a repossessed property being offered at an unbelievably low price and I fell for the estate agent's sales pitch when he told me that he had queues of people waiting to buy it and that I needed to move fast.

So I took it and discovered later that it had been on the market for eight months and was a jerry-built, former council house, riddled with damp.

But worst of all, it was over three miles from the university. That might not matter in London, provided the property is near an underground station.

But in an area served only by infrequent buses and where there is a good supply of rental properties within close walking distance of the university, it was a serious mistake.

Nevertheless, I decided to make the best of it and had the property fully refurbished. It was a large property with good-sized bedrooms, two bathrooms and lots of off-road parking, ideal for students.

However, there was nothing I could do about its location.

The university advertised it for me and I started collecting students from their halls of residence, and taking them to view. I remember on numerous occasions, talking up the property en route, saying how lovely it was and how good the bus service was etc, hoping they didn't notice how far we were travelling.

But you can't easily con a student, and they never called back!

I soon began to think that it would not let. Be warned: there is nothing worse for a landlord than an empty property.

After six months you have to start paying council tax on it and you have to keep visiting to make sure that it hasn't been taken over by squatters. It starts to smell and decay, and then it becomes difficult to sell.

It costs you money to keep it and you invariably lose money if you sell it too soon. This was my predicament.

And then the phone rang.

It was a head teacher friend of mine. He had just started hosting a post-graduate teacher-training course for mature students at his school and needed to find accommodation for the students. Knowing I had student houses, he called to see if I could help.

Could I help! These students, all of whom had cars or motorbikes, didn't mind travelling a few miles. Coming from different parts of the country none of them knew the area, and relied on staff at the school to find them suitable accommodation before they arrived.

At the same time, I was also approached by twin sisters, both fitness fanatics, who wanted to share a room and seemed to love the idea of running three miles in to university every day and three miles back, no matter what the weather.

The gods were on my side. So, despite my awful mistake, I struck lucky.

But three years later, when the teacher-training course folded, and the twins ran off to their careers with never a backward glance, I sold the property, made a good profit and bought something much closer to the university. Lesson learned.

The Fifteen Minute Rule

Rule number one is that the vast majority of students really don't like to travel. They would rather take a smaller, more expensive, house five minutes from the university than a large one that's twenty minutes away.

My rule of thumb has been that nothing should be more than a fifteen-minute walk from the site the students use.

The further away it is the bigger and better it should be. It should have off-road parking and/or a bike shed or should be very close to a good public transport connection.

Buying a property further away than this, especially one with small rooms and nowhere for cars or bikes, is a non-starter.

Then again, when you are researching your area by walking the streets, make sure you go back there at night.

What may seem to be a pleasant street in broad daylight could transform after dark into the hub of the red light area or the staging post for gentlemen trading little packets in dark alleyways.

Your students will not thank you for putting them in a street like that, no matter how nice the property or how close to the university.

They might well cite 'non-disclosure' on your part as grounds for getting out of a contract if they have to run the gauntlet of pimps, prostitutes, punters and pushers, as they wend their way home from lectures every evening.

In my own city there is a clear geographical demarcation that defines safe and non-safe areas. East of the university is a no-no but anything west is fine. A similar demarcation is common in inner cities through the UK.

Prospective tenants and their parents will often ask whether the area is safe and whether there is a likelihood of a break-in.

Provided you have not bought a property in a notorious crime area, you can answer the first part of that question reassuringly.

Burglaries

As to burglaries, my answer is always that anyone in any area can suffer a burglary. My own home has suffered several in the last twenty years, and I live in a very pleasant leafy lane.

One might suggest that 'posh' houses are burgled more often anyway.

Not true. For some peculiar reason, student houses are a prime target, even though the best the burglar can hope for is perhaps a computer and an iPod.

That is because most petty burglars are drug users and opportunists who, desperate to fund their next fix, will break into any house near to their own back yard.

So I have to answer the question honestly. Break-ins are rare but there are a number of measures that tenants can take to prevent them.

Determined burglars, however, are seldom put off by locks and burglar alarms. They just smash their way in, and grab what they can.

Tony's Tips

- When starting your student property business, it is best to live locally.

- Build up a team of regular, reliable contractors.

- Research your market carefully before buying – talk to students.

- Always go for quality – students are very choosy.

- Overseas students are a growing market, but put pressure on your local university to guarantee rents.

- Choose a location as close as possible to the university, or close to good public transport links.

- Avoid 'unsafe' areas.

Chapter 5

Buying the Right Property

The first student property I bought was a pleasant, well-built, five-bedroom semi within a ten-minute walk of the university. Sounds perfect? Not at all!

Now I wouldn't give it a second glance! Why? Because four of the bedrooms were small singles!

In those days, that didn't matter, because there was a shortage of student properties and just as long as it was warm and safe and dry, students were delighted to sign on the dotted line. But now there's a lot of competition so it's essential to buy a property that you can be confident will be easy to let.

What Students Want

So what do students want? Double bedrooms! And a lot of other things too, which will be dealt with later in this chapter.

But first you need to find the right property. Having identified the areas and streets where you want to be, forget the others, and start your search.

You are looking for a property in which all the bedrooms are ideally big enough to house a double bed, desk, wardrobe, chest of drawers, one or two chairs and still have a reasonable amount of floor space.

Older houses in urban areas often have one bedroom that is much smaller than the others. These should be avoided if possible because these rooms are hard to let, even when groups of friends are taking the house, and virtually impossible to let if you are renting out the house room by room.

Many students will have come from small rooms like these in the hall of residence or even back home, and one of the big attractions to a student in taking a house is to have a big room.

Provided there are no more than five tenants, one bathroom and kitchen is OK. But if you can get a house with a second toilet and even a separate shower room, that is a big bonus and will be very attractive to prospective tenants.

Years ago, provided the bedrooms were of a good size, I used to make the sitting room into an extra bedroom. But students these days like sitting rooms, and even though you don't get rent from a sitting room, you will find it difficult, if not impossible, to let a house that doesn't have one – and your local accreditation scheme may demand it anyway.

Sitting Rooms are Very Important

Provided the bedrooms are of a good size, you can get away with a sitting room that is just about big enough to seat everyone in front of the television. To have no sitting room at all is to risk having a house that will not let. A very large kitchen with dining/communal area is a poor substitute.

Assuming there is a sitting room, kitchens don't need to be big provided they are well laid out. Beware of buying an older property where a toilet or bathroom opens directly from a kitchen (which contravenes regulations in most accreditation schemes), or where there is no escape from the downstairs bathroom at the back of the house other than through the kitchen (which contravenes fire regulations).

Move-in Condition vs. Refurbishment

The condition of the property you want to buy will depend on how much you are willing to spend on refurbishment and the amount of time you have to get it ready. Unless the property already meets standards specified in your local accreditation scheme you will almost certainly need to have it re-wired and have other safety features added.

It is therefore a false economy to buy a house where you're paying over the odds for the seller's decorating and cleaning skills. You will have to redecorate and clean anyway after you have finished taking up floorboards, gouging holes in plaster and replacing leaking shower trays.

In my experience, it's far better to buy a property needing full refurbishment. These come much cheaper anyway and you can be sure that the work is done properly and to the right standard from the start. This will then obviate the need for anything more than normal maintenance for the following ten or more years.

Bear in mind that the property you are buying is one that you will need to sell one day. Ask yourself why it has been on the market for so long and make sure that whatever you do to it makes it a more sellable proposition.

Do You Need a Garden?

Some landlords prefer to buy properties without gardens in areas where gardens are the norm, the idea being to cut out garden maintenance.

I believe this is a mistake, because keeping a garden smart need not be expensive. Prospective tenants like the idea of somewhere to have summer barbecues, and it makes the property more marketable when the time comes eventually to sell.

The Right Time to Buy

The time of year when you buy is quite important. Spring is the busiest time when lots of new properties come on to the market, and you will be competing with other buyers, and probably have to pay top prices.

The last thing you want is to get into a 'closed bid' system where there are a lot of other people after the property and who are willing to pay over the asking price.

Given that completion of a purchase that started in the spring might not happen until July or even August, you are then left with very little time to get your property ready and have it tenanted by the start of the university year in late September.

So, spring would not be a good time to buy unless you were buying a property that was already a student house, met all the safety requirements, was up and running, and just needed to be cleaned.

But if you are buying a property that needs work done on it, a better option is to buy around Christmas time. This is the dead end of the year when owners are desperate to get rid of properties that have probably been on the market for months so they are ready to accept very low offers.

The deal will be completed in February or March, giving you six months to get it ready, and there is nothing to stop you conducting viewings while work is in progress.

I have let several houses that were little more than building sites because the students viewing liked the idea of being the first into a newly decorated, 'fresh' house.

Example

On one occasion, an all-female group made several visits to check on progress. I was pleased to give them a written guarantee that deposits would be returned in full, plus a penalty of £50 each, if the property wasn't ready by a certain date. Needless to say, it was ready in plenty of time! They even got to choose the colour of the carpets.

Finding a Property

Your first port of call when searching for a house will probably be the property pages of the local newspaper, but bear in mind that these pages do not contain every property on the estate agents' books.

For that, you will need to look at their websites or visit their premises. Tell them you are an 'investor' (estate agents love investors!) and the type of property you're looking for. They will offer to put you on their mailing list, so be specific about your location.

Even then they'll probably end up sending you everything that comes on to their books, or not send you anything at all, so be persistent and keep phoning them and get to know the name of the person in their office who seems most on the ball. Eventually, they will start phoning you.

Watch out for the Parasites

The type of 'agent' you should avoid at all costs are the ones who pose as auctioneers or estate agents, or who offer to build portfolios for you. If you do an online search for auctioneers or estate agents you'll come across many websites where you're required to 'register' your details.

You think you're registering with a bona fide company but actually you are registering with a parasite – a company that trades off the back of established auctioneers and estate agents. What happens next is that you start getting phone calls from these 'agents' who offer to find the type of property you want and expect a fat fee in advance.

All they are doing is taking over your search for you and making you pay through the nose for what you could easily do yourself at no cost.

Moreover, they rarely pay close attention to what you really want. They will either waste your time with a lot of unsuitable properties or, worse, persuade you to make a purchase that you'll later regret.

The 'agents' who construct portfolios are even worse because they actually buy properties on your behalf, gambling on your not knowing the real value before selling them on to you.

Example

Last year I was selling a small, terraced, three-bedroom house. Since it was recently refurbished and therefore in very clean condition, I was asking the top market price for that type of property in that location. I was selling the property because the third bedroom was very small and proving hard to let.

I had a call from one of these portfolio companies who offered me the asking price. I later discovered that within days of buying from me, the company had sold on the property to a London purchaser at 20% above what they had paid me. Because it was a cash deal, no independent valuation was involved.

No doubt the London buyer didn't realise that the price paid was 20% above market value and that the property would be hard to let. I presume the portfolio company gave him a completely different story.

I drive past that house every day, and notice that it still has not been let, seven months after the sale. I presume that, being in London, the new owner has placed the property with a local letting agent who is not marketing it vigorously enough. If you want to lose money, this is the way to do it.

Property Auctions

So, having avoided the charlatans and parasites, another option in your search for a property is auctions. For these, you must have your finance arranged in advance, because you are committed on the fall of the hammer and have to complete the purchase usually within 14 or 28 days.

Auctions used to be a good source for cheap properties but in the last few years, prices at auctions have often been higher than buying through estate agents so, again, go during midwinter if you want the best bargains.

One thing to be wary about when using auctions is that the majority of properties being offered are there because they have something wrong with them and couldn't sell on the High Street.

If this is something you can handle within your budget, like a full new damp course or a re-roof, then go ahead and you might get a bargain. But if you think there is something structurally wrong with the place, exercise extreme caution.

You will get the chance to view auction properties at specified times, so go with a tape measure, torch and spirit level (to see if floors are level). If you have a friendly, competent, local builder, take him with you with the promise that he will get the work if you buy the property. He will tell you immediately if there are major problems.

Ask the agents if a structural survey has been done and whether there are any known problems. They are required by law to give you a truthful answer.

If you decide to go to the auction, make contact before bidding starts with the solicitor acting for the seller. She or he will tell you if all the local searches are clear. You don't want to buy a property that will lose value because a new fly-over is about to be constructed over its roof.

Decide on Your Top Price

Once you are reasonably sure the property has no problems you can't address and you want to bid, decide what it's worth to you before bidding starts. Ignore the guide price put on it by the auctioneer – it's meaningless and bears little relationship to the price achieved.

The price you're prepared to pay is based on what you feel the real market value of such a property would be when fully refurbished, less the amount you will have to spend on it (overestimate this by 20% because it always costs more than you think) but governed by what you can genuinely afford.

The resulting figure is your top price, and stick to it, no matter what happens. Don't get carried away by the enthusiasm of other bidders or the excitement of the occasion – you'll live to regret it. If the bidding goes past your price, leave it – there will always be other, better properties another day.

Check Out the Local Council

Another source for properties is the local council. They often have an estate department that sells council-owned properties of all types and sizes. Some of these are surprisingly good and in perfect locations.

I once bought a Victorian property that had been the caretaker's house for a local school before the school went private. The house therefore became surplus to the council's requirements and was put up for sale.

It had been well maintained for years, and so was relatively cheap to upgrade for student occupation. So call your local council and ask them to send you lists of what they are selling.

The Last Resort

But if you are trying to buy during a period when there is almost nothing on the market, your last resort is shank's pony. Walk the streets and look out for signs put up by people who are selling privately to avoid estate agents' fees. Even knock on a few doors to ask if a property might be sold in the near future.

Opposite one property I bought was a completely derelict house with trees growing through the windows. It was in a prime location and owning two properties close to one another is always very convenient and economical. I put a note through the door of the derelict property asking if it was for sale and, a few weeks later had a call from the owner asking if I would like to view.

Had he not replied, I could have found out his name by going to the local council or the land registry. In the event I didn't buy that one because it was built over an old mine shaft! Due to all the foliage on the walls I hadn't spotted huge diagonal zigzagging cracks running down from the windows – a sure sign of a serious subsidence.

Arranging Finance

OK, so you've found the perfect student property in the perfect location and now you need to raise the money to buy it. Of course, it's always best to sort this out before you start your property search so that you know how much you can afford.

But now that buy-to-let lenders are falling over themselves to give away money, it is not unreasonable these days to find the property first and then apply for the loan.

By far the easiest and cheapest way of raising money is to re-mortgage your own home because the only thing the lender will need to know is whether it is now worth comfortably more than the total amount being borrowed against it.

You can use your current lender or take out a second mortgage with a different lender, but whichever you choose, shop around because the market is very competitive and lenders will fight for your business.

If you are choosing a repayment mortgage, borrow as much as you can afford over the longest possible period to keep the monthly repayments as low as possible.

Monthly payments on interest-only mortgages are even lower, but that is because you are not repaying the capital and you will be required to repay the full amount borrowed when you eventually sell the property. Hopefully, the value of the property will have risen considerably by then, so the amount repayable will be a much smaller percentage of the property value than when the loan was taken out.

Buy-to-let Mortgages

If you are taking out a mortgage on the property you are buying to let, you can also choose to have a repayment or interest-only mortgage. The lender, however, will only lend you up to 85% of its valuation. They will also want to know how much rent you will be taking each month and what type of tenancy agreement you are using.

Many lenders insist there should be a joint tenancy agreement for the whole property and seem unable to come to terms with the concept of individual tenancy agreements for a shared house, as is the case with most student lets.

The Problem with Joint Tenancy Agreements

I always give students individual tenancy agreements. This is because a joint tenancy agreement means that all tenants are 'jointly and severally' responsible for one another's rent. Not only can a student not afford to pay for a defaulting friend but the guarantors are usually most unwilling to guarantee anyone other than their own offspring.

It really is time the lenders came to terms with this and understood that individual tenancy agreements still have clauses covering collective responsibility for the property. They are also much easier to enforce.

I wrote recently to one of these lenders, which had been used by a number of people who have bought properties from me. Each time there was a hold-up because the lender wanted to see a joint tenancy agreement.

I asked why they insisted on joint tenancy agreements, given that individual agreements in shared houses defined collective responsibilities in exactly the same way. The only difference is that individuals are responsible only for their own rent.

I explained that students were unhappy about this, that their guarantors (usually a parent) were unwilling to guarantee the rent of other tenants, and that individual agreements are much easier to enforce.

I received a very delayed reply from the Head of PR (complete with a disclaimer, telling me the reply was confidential! – to whom?) simply re-stating their policy, which was to insist on single agreement.

The lender said this was "fair, and is transparent to both student and landlord". I wrote again asking what was the risk in having separate tenancy agreements. He wrote regretting that he had nothing further to add on the subject. So much for transparency.

Choosing a Lender

When choosing a lender you will find a wide array of mortgage packages. There is no quick way to choose the best other than by reading carefully through the small print.

Some offer free valuations, legal fees and other goodies, including cash-back, whereas others add the cost of the various fees to the mortgage, meaning you end up paying much more in the long run when the interest charges have been added.

Mortgages offering significant discounts over the first few years seem attractive. However, after the discount period has ended the monthly payments can rise very sharply, thus cutting your monthly profit to the bone.

Personally, I favour tracker mortgages that are pegged to the bank base rate from the start. It is then easier to budget your rental income against mortgage payments that don't fluctuate wildly.

Read the Small Print

When taking out the loan, look carefully at the conditions and ask supplementary questions, making sure to get answers in writing. In particular, you should take careful note of the charges and penalties that are applied when you redeem the loan.

Early Redemption Penalties

Most loans have an early redemption penalty period, which is usually three years. If you sell the property (and thus redeem the loan) within that period, you are hit with a big penalty charge. Most lenders also apply various 'administrative charges' for supplying documents or for other forms of communication with you. You might expect this to be part of the service you are paying for – it is not!

Recently I decided to sell four properties on which I had taken loans only three years previously with the same lender. After redemption, I had to ask the company each time to send me a completion statement showing what interest had been charged, and confirming that they would stop drawing on the monthly direct debit. In one case they took an extra month, which I had to claim back.

Watch your bank account like a hawk!

Other lenders usually send these statements out as routine. In the case of all four mortgages, I was charged redemption penalties I didn't expect.

The first was a charge of 5% of the total of the loan, for redeeming within the three-year period. There had been some confusion about the date the loan had started, with the result that, according to the lender, I had redeemed twelve days before the full three years had expired.

Despite the fact that I was so near the end of the three-year period, and had three other mortgages with this company, they wouldn't budge and insisted on retaining the full 5% (which, in this case, was £3,300!).

I pointed out that other lenders had shown more sympathy and flexibility in similar circumstances and asked if we could agree on a more reasonable sum. But they replied saying "we have to hedge our exposure entirely, and early repayment of such funds incurs additional interest costs, which would result in a loss for the Company".

I found it difficult to believe that the Company stood to lose £3,300 as a result of my redeeming twelve days early!

The same lender also applied two months' extra interest charge on the three other mortgages I was redeeming, on the grounds that I had not given them two months' notice of the redemption. In each case, my solicitor had written well before the two-month period telling them that the properties were being sold, and asked for a redemption statement.

When I pointed this out to the lender, they replied saying they considered the solicitor's letter was "for accounting purposes only" and did not constitute proper notice.

Nowhere in the conditions attached to the loan could I find a definition of the 'proper notice' they required, so I persisted with my claim that this interest should be paid back. Eventually, the lender gave in, describing its climb-down as an "act of goodwill".

I have learnt never to accept the rulings of these big companies, and I go on making a nuisance of myself for as long as possible.

In most cases the companies give in, discovering an unknown sub-clause that allows a face-saving change of mind, or simply citing 'act of goodwill' as a reason for giving in to my persistence.

The real reason is, of course, fear of adverse publicity in a market that is extremely competitive.

Valuations

When you have applied for your mortgage, the lender will then instruct a firm of surveyors to undertake a valuation. Having been present at these on numerous occasions, I can say with complete confidence that I have never seen such a wide array of practices among people who are supposed to have undergone rigorous professional training and are required to assess a property against published, objective criteria.

Some valuers seem to have a mission in life to do the very best they can to obstruct the sale of a property. They are the Scrooges in the conveyancing process. I could fill another book with tales about them but I will restrict myself to three experiences to illustrate the way some of them operate.

A few years ago I was re-mortgaging two properties, using two different lenders. Each appointed different companies to undertake the valuations. The purpose of these valuations is to reassure the lender that the money they are advancing can be recouped by selling the property in the event of the borrower defaulting on the mortgage repayments.

They are not full structural surveys, or even home-buyers' surveys. The valuer is expected to check that the property is in a reasonably sound condition and to arrive at a market value.

In both of these cases, I was borrowing only £50,000 against properties which were worth well over £150,000 each, so all the valuers had to do was reassure the lender that they would get their money back if the property had to be sold.

Case One

In this case, the valuer went in with an array of rules, ladders and meters, spending over two hours at the property. He gave it a derisory value of £75,000 and recommended that specialist reports be obtained for damp, timber, drains and tree encroachment.

In other words, he was passing the buck. Some valuers call for all these supplementary reports to cover their backs in the event of a problem developing with the property at a later date.

But what they don't understand is that this causes a major bureaucratic blockage in the sale process. The lender usually won't proceed without these supplementary reports, or imposes a retention of several thousand pounds, until hypothetical remedial work is carried out. In most cases, this work is not even necessary and is a 'worst-case scenario' supposition on the part of the valuer.

In this particular case, I had to call out four sets of specialists, all of whom gave the property a clean bill of health. But not only did these extra inspections delay matters by three crucial weeks, during which I lost out on another property I was intending to buy with the proceeds of the re-mortgage, they cost me an additional £800 in fees.

A month later, the identical house next door, which was in a much poorer condition, was sold for £185,000. So much for 'market value'.

Case Two

The second example is of a valuer at the other end of the spectrum. I knew that the house he was going to look at had a problem with its roof and I fully expected him to include that in his report.

It was raining on the day I met him at the property and he dashed in, head down, through the front door without ever looking up at the roof. He stood with me in the hallway asking a few questions about the tenancies. He glanced around him, commented on how nice the Minton tile floor was in the hallway and then said everything looked fine.

He left within three minutes and his report valued the property at £175,000. Had I been selling that property rather than re-mortgaging it, the buyer would have bought a property with a defective roof.

I hasten to add that the second of these two examples is less common than the first. It is much more likely that you'll get a valuer who seriously undervalues the property and who calls for additional reports.

If your finances are tight and you're relying on a fair valuation to raise the required 85% mortgage, a low valuation can scupper your purchase before you even start – and then you will still be left with legal and arrangement fees to pay.

My third example nearly did just that.

Case Three

I was selling a six-bedroom house with garage and large garden at a big discount to a landlord friend. I was confident it was worth over £160,000, but we had agreed on a sale price of £145,000. This was a private sale, the property was empty but furnished. The previous tenants had just vacated it and it had not been advertised on the open market.

The valuer was another of the quick-in, quicker-out brigade. When the valuation came through it was for £115,000! My friend and I both went into shock as no house on that road was worth less than £140,000, and this was the biggest and best.

When we read the valuation in detail, our shock turned to dismay and then to anger. The valuer claimed he didn't have proper access during his visit to inspect for damp (rubbish! – he hadn't even tried testing for damp, and the downstairs rooms were all open and unoccupied). He added that the house was small and had been on the market for a long time.

It soon became clear that he had reported on the wrong house and so an angry three-page letter went from the buyer's solicitor to the lender.

A less savvy buyer would have just accepted the report and probably backed out of the deal, having wasted money on fees. Despite the solicitor's letter, the valuer refused to admit his mistake and so my friend had to pay for a second valuation from another firm and, surprise, surprise, the house was valued at £165,000.

Solicitors

If you are intending to build up a property portfolio over the course of time, it is essential that you find a good solicitor to handle your conveyancing swiftly, efficiently and cheaply.

I have had the same guy, Derek, acting for me for twenty years, and have recommended him to numerous friends and relatives. Just because you live in London, it doesn't follow that you need to employ a top-charging London solicitor!

Conveyancing is all done from a desk, so the solicitor doesn't need to be in the same town as the properties you are buying. My solicitor has bought properties for me and my family in all parts of England and at a fraction of the cost of some of the big, high-profile city firms.

That said, he is excellent at what he does and knows the standards I require. If I say I want exchange and completion on the same day within three weeks, it happens, and if there are any delays beyond his control, he calls me before I need to call him, and keeps me informed.

Remember Who's Boss

Many purchasers seem to be afraid of their solicitors, and forget that it is they who are giving the instructions, not the other way around.

I was recently selling some properties to a man who had been messing me around for months, causing one delay after the other. At the last minute, he decided to go on holiday. We knew his mortgage offer was in and both the estate agent acting for me and my solicitor were pressing for an exchange of contracts.

Meanwhile, other cash buyers were lining up, so I was faced with the choice of staying with the time-waster or accepting another offer.

We gave his solicitor a final deadline for exchange, to which his response was that he couldn't exchange that week because his fax machine had broken down! If I ran a competition for the best excuses offered for delays in conveyancing, I'm sure this one would be in the top ten!

So I went with one of the cash buyers and exchanged within three days. When Mr Time-Waster returned from his holiday to find he had lost the properties, he was more than a little upset. Hard cheese!

A married couple, buying their first buy-to-let from me, chose a pedantic dinosaur of a solicitor who did everything by the book. He even seemed to invent books along the way, and that way was travelled at snail's pace. I'm sure his letters had been signed with a quill!

When he discovered that the property was going to be tenanted, he chose to get involved in every tiny detail of the tenancy arrangements. He asked me, for example, if the contractors I used, to which I referred in the tenancy agreements, were part of the sale.

I replied, explaining that my builder's wife might have something to say if she knew I was selling him with one of my properties.

He also wanted formal ID of all the tenants (who hadn't moved in and were away on their summer vacations). He seemed hugely worried about whether the furniture was fireproof and whether safety certificates were up to date – all matters for the new owner to attend to prior to the tenants moving in, and nothing to do with the sale of the house.

Of course, all these safety measures were in place, but each letter was taking up more time, being sent first to my solicitor, on to me, back to my solicitor and then back to the buyer's solicitor (so much for email!)

These questions went on and on, week after week, until I reached the end of my tether. I said I refused to answer any more questions about the tenancies, or to provide any more assurances, and that if exchange and completion did not happen within seven days, the deal was off.

It happened. The purchasers were much relieved and obviously should have told their solicitor to stop meddling weeks before but, being new to the game, they tended to regard him with a certain mystique and reverence normally reserved for those professionals who deal with matters far beyond the understanding of mere mortals, like brain surgeons and car mechanics.

Attention to Detail

At the other extreme, beware solicitors who pay no attention to detail until the last moment – these people can cause the biggest last-minute delays of all.

What happens here is the buyer's solicitor's office sends out all the pre-sale enquiry forms to the seller, and also sends off for searches to the local authority without the solicitor having any input at all.

When the answers to these enquiries come in, what the solicitor should be doing is checking through and following up with any supplementary enquiries. But what often happens is that the answers are filed away by a secretary, and only looked at by the solicitor when the mortgage offer comes in.

This is bad practice because, instead of then going straight to exchange of contracts, the solicitor starts writing endless letters to the seller's solicitor asking questions which should have been asked weeks earlier.

I recently sold a property to a buyer who had problems with his lender and, after wasting two months, he decided to switch lenders and start again. His solicitors said that all the searches and pre-sale enquiries were in, so matters could proceed as soon as the mortgage was offered.

So we waited and waited while a second valuation was done and then eventually, the mortgage offer arrived. As soon as I heard the news I asked if we could exchange and complete the following week. It then transpired that the solicitor was faxing across a number of supplementary enquiries about planning consent, gas and electrical certificates, and the tenancies, all of which could and should have been dealt with weeks earlier.

This delayed matters by a further four weeks, resulting in the whole process being extended to four months. During this period, the property I was selling had increased in value by at least 5%, but had I asked for an increase in the sale price, the sale would have collapsed because the buyer was mortgaging to his limit. So his solicitor's last-minute attention to detail cost me dear.

Insurance

As soon as you have exchanged sale contracts, you need to insure the property because you are committed to complete the sale thereafter and, should it burn down in the meantime, it will be your loss, not the seller's.

Some lenders will try to persuade you to use their own insurance schemes, which are almost always more expensive than insurance you can get elsewhere.

Even if you insist on using your own insurer, they will ask to see evidence that you have insured the property to the value they have placed on it.

The sum for which you insure a property is based on the cost of rebuilding it.

Bear in mind that property prices have risen much faster than building costs in recent years. Even if a property burns to the ground, you still have the land.

So when negotiating rebuilding costs with the insurer, argue that the market value is almost certainly much higher than the rebuilding costs, so your premiums will be lower.

Shop Around

As with everything else, it's best to shop around for insurance and to ask for bulk discounts where you are insuring several properties with the same insurer. Most will give you a single insurance policy listing all the separate properties.

While this results in cheaper premiums, it can also have implications on your claims record. Most insurers will not penalise you for making up to two claims within a twelve-month period.

While this may sound reasonable for one property, it is less so if you have 20 properties on the same policy. So you need to ask about this when choosing your policy.

You don't want to be in a position where your premiums double following a spate of local burglaries that might affect three or more of your properties in one year.

Check to see what else the policy is offering you in terms of public liability (essential) and loss of rent (less so, unless you anticipate yours being one of a tiny number of student houses that catch fire each year, resulting in the tenants having to move out).

Contents Insurance

I do not insure the contents of my properties because thieves rarely steal double beds and wardrobes, so why pay the additional premiums?

But I do advise my tenants to insure their own belongings. This can sometimes be appended to their parents' own home insurance. If not, I advise them to take out one policy between them rather than individually, which is cheaper.

I also make it clear it's up to them to insure the freezer contents in the event of a breakdown. When freezers have gone wrong in the past, it always seemed to be when tenants said only the day before they had bought hundreds of pounds worth of frozen food and now it has all been ruined. I don't think so.

Utilities

Unless you are buying property that is already tenanted, you will need to open accounts in your name with the various utilities to cover the period between purchase and letting while you are doing renovations.

As a matter of policy, I always pay the water rates in my properties, and include the charge in the rent (currently less than one pound per tenant per week). This is because student tenancies do not usually last the full twelve months, and water companies bill not monthly, but twice yearly.

If tenants don't pay the bills, the water companies make a charge against the property that the owner ends up paying anyway. So I give the water companies my home address for billing.

But in the case of gas and electricity, I NEVER give my home address because once they know the name and location of the landlord, they will always revert to that information whenever tenants leave owing money.

They are notorious for ignoring letters of explanation, their systems being entirely automated, with the result that non payment always progresses very quickly to the appointment of debt collectors and threats of court action. Getting them off your back is a nightmare, and one to be avoided.

So, having opened an account for a property that I intend to let, I give them that address for bills and then close the account on the day the new tenants move in, giving my final readings and the tenants' start readings simultaneously.

I do not give a forwarding address for the final bill but, instead, I go to collect it a few days later. Thereafter, the gas and electricity accounts remain in the tenants' names. If a property is empty between tenancies during a summer period, estimated bills start arriving, sometimes addressed to the old tenant, and sometimes to the 'new occupier'.

I bin all of these, and the new tenants provide a start reading when they move in. Given that the property has been vacant between tenancies, there won't have been any consumption of gas or electricity, so the previous final reading should be the same as the start reading for the new tenants.

As for telephone and broadband, I leave that entirely to the tenants to organise. Most properties in urban areas have a broadband connection outside the front door and the companies concerned will usually take the cables through any room requested by the tenant at no charge.

Given the growing demand for wireless internet, you may wish to consider providing that as a basic facility in your property. It costs very little per month, and will certainly help to market your property.

Council Tax

As soon as you have purchased a property, you become liable for the council tax charges on it.

An empty, unfurnished property is given full exemption for up to six months but if it has already been exempted for the same reason in the months prior to your buying it, then you may have very little time left before you are expected to pay council tax.

Unless you are undertaking substantial renovation that renders the property uninhabitable (the Council will ask for evidence of this, and may even come to inspect) there will be council tax to be paid.

Student Exemptions

As soon as your student tenants move in, however, you can claim exemptions. Some councils insist that the landlord remains 'the responsible person' for making the claim where shared houses are in multiple occupation. Other councils are happy for the tenants to make the claim.

The current rules for exemptions are that where all tenants are full-time students, there is a 100% discount. But if one tenant is not full-time the discount reduces to 25% and if two are not full time, then there is no discount at all and the full amount of council tax levied on the property must be paid. This will be billed to the 'responsible person', so make sure your tenancy agreement makes it clear that where council tax is payable, the landlord can re-charge the tenants.

The irony is that part-time students are usually the poorest of all because they do not qualify for full financial support. They have to subsidise their income by working longer hours in pubs and factories than their full-time student house mates.

Warn your tenants that if any of them become part-time students, or give up their studies and decide to claim benefits, the benefits office will automatically notify the council tax office, and a bill for council tax will then arrive on your doormat!

Make it clear to the tenants both verbally and in the tenancy agreement, that any council tax due as a result of their change of status or through claiming benefits will be the responsibility of the tenant concerned. The only problem with this is that, according to the Council, it is your responsibility, so you then have the unenviable task of having to collect it.

The document councils accept as proof that a student is full time is either a copy of the enrolment form or an agreed pro-forma Council Tax letter that universities now issue to students specifically for the purpose of getting council tax exemption.

Both of these documents state clearly the number of contact hours in the student's course, and whether the course is full time.

Councils usually send out renewal notices in early October to coincide with enrolment dates. If your Council insists that the landlord makes the claim, then you must place a large envelope in the property asking the tenants to place a copy of their enrolment form or council tax letter in it by a certain date. They can then either post it to you or have you collect it. You then send this to the council with the application form. If you hear nothing more, then the exemption has been awarded.

Some Councils have the annoying habit of sending out new bills for council tax as soon as the end date of a particular student's course has arrived. This means you are then required to let them know when those students have left the property so that the exemption can continue.

Other councils are happy to let the exemption run for the full twelve months, even though the student courses will have finished in May or June. Making these applications, and responding to the various demands of the council, is an onerous task. It is one I feel should not fall to the landlord, because he is being put in the position of being an unpaid tax collector.

If some Councils can deal directly with tenants, why not all? It also seems unfair that Council Tax is not levied on student halls of residence, so halls managers are not required to submit exemption applications, as is required of private landlords.

A few years ago, three students occupying one of my flats decided to stay on after qualifying and to work locally. I warned them that they would have to pay council tax now that they were no longer students, and they were fine about it.

Since they were all adult workers with, in this case, a shared tenancy agreement, I assumed the Council would be willing to bill them directly. Not so! The Council insisted on inspecting the property and interviewing the tenants!

They concluded that, because the tenants were unrelated, and had locks on their bedroom doors, the flat was in multiple occupation and I was therefore still the responsible person.

I appealed and, months later, sat before a tribunal of local worthies – all councillors from a neighbouring council, so hardly an independent group. They listened carefully and politely to my argument that these three people had come to me as an established group of friends two years earlier. I said they lived as a family, shared communal areas and housekeeping (just as all my student tenants do) and that even natural families often have locks on bedroom doors.

I received a letter a week later telling me that the tribunal had decided to uphold the ruling, so i lost the appeal.

Tony's Tips

- Look for properties where all bedrooms are big enough for double beds.

- Houses needing a full refurbishment are cheaper and a better investment in the long run.

- Avoid 'agents' who find or buy properties for you.

- Auctions near Christmas are the best place for cheap houses but beware of structural or planning problems.

- Shop around for the best mortgage deal – tracker mortgages are preferable.

- Always fight your corner if landed with extra mortgage charges.

- Challenge valuations if you think they are wrong.

- Remember: you instruct solicitors, they don't instruct you.

- When taking out insurance, argue that re-building costs may be less than market value.

- Never give your home address to utility companies.

- Make sure that tenants know they are responsible for paying Council Tax if they do not qualify for exemption.

Chapter 6

Getting Your Property Ready

Expecting the Unexpected

The day you collect the keys for your new property is one of mixed feelings. On the one hand you are now the proud owner of an investment property, and perhaps you feel you are now making it in the world. On the other hand, you may be filled with foreboding if, on a cold, damp day in January, you open the front door for the first time and are greeted by the musty smell of a property that has been locked up for several months and is dark, dirty, and unwelcoming.

As you walk around, you'll notice things you hadn't seen when the property was warm, light and full of furniture back in the autumn – the rising damp in the front room, the condensation pouring off the windows, ominous dark patches on the chimney breast, copious quantities of black mould on the bathroom ceiling, mouse droppings on the kitchen shelves, the mountains of rubbish in the loft and the cellar – and you suddenly wonder if you will ever let the place.

Welcome to the trials and tribulations of the landlord!

Even in properties that appeared to be in tip-top condition when viewed and surveyed, you will always find things that you hadn't previously spotted, because furniture conceals a multitude of sins, and fitted carpets even more so.

If you have paid for an expensive survey don't expect him to have lifted the carpets, because he won't. And if the loft isn't easily accessible, he won't have looked in there either.

So it's best always to expect the worst and then you'll be pleasantly surprised when things turn out better than expected. This is why I prefer to buy properties that are in need of total refurbishment. I can then take into account the cost of, for example, replacement windows, full damp course, full re-wire, new kitchen, new bathroom, roof repairs, new central heating system etc, when negotiating the purchase price.

Even then, I occasionally get surprises. A few years ago I bought a house that needed all of the above doing, except that it had a new, top-of-the-range, condensing boiler.

On entering the property on the day of completion, I found ugly twisted crimped-off copper pipes hanging from the wall where the boiler had been! My solicitor was quickly on to it and came back to me with the story that the property had been broken into after exchange of contracts but before completion and the boiler ripped from the wall.

After a few enquiries of my own, I ascertained that no break-in had been reported to the police and that the owner had been refurbishing another property, which included – surprise, surprise – the installation of a condensing boiler.

He ignored several letters from me, so I had an identical boiler installed and then took him to the small claims court for reimbursement of my costs. He failed to respond to the court papers so I was awarded judgment by default.

The problem with all these small claims cases is that getting judgment is the easy part – getting the money is extremely difficult.

But in this case, the man lived in a pleasant suburban house with two nice cars in the driveway. When the bailiff called him to say one of his cars was about to be towed away, he rushed down to the bailiff's office and handed over a wad of cash.

Finding Your Contractors

One of the reasons I went into property was because I was a DIY enthusiast and always enjoyed hammering, screwing and slopping on paint. But even if you don't know your ballcock from your architrave, you can still save yourself a lot of money by doing many of the non-skilled jobs yourself.

The first thing I would recommend is putting a tow-bar on your car and getting a trailer. Like most things, I learned this the hard way after attending an auction in my early days, and picking up a lot of very good, cheap furniture. I then found that the cost of hiring a lorry to transport the stuff was twice as much as I'd paid for the furniture.

So I hunted for a trailer and bought an old caravan base on which I constructed sides and a back and put on a lights kit bought from my local branch of Halfords. The whole thing cost me less than £100 and lasted fifteen years.

The money it saved me over that time ran into many thousands of pounds, given that I used it to transport everything from furniture to and between properties, to taking rubbish to the municipal dump.

Eventually, its axles seized up, so then I felt justified in replacing it with a brand new, very posh, aluminium trailer, which is lighter and even bigger. I also invested in an old van to save the boot of my car from the damage being caused by carrying tools, paint and cleaning materials.

Clearing Out the Rubbish

So, the first thing you'll need to do in your property is to clear out the rubbish. I have never yet bought a property that didn't have accumulated rubbish, old carpets, broken furniture, sheds full of unwanted garden items and so on.

Before any work can start, it all needs to be removed. Pay someone to do it and it may set you back a few hundred pounds. Rope in a friend or family member and it costs only the price of the petrol to the dump, provided you have a trailer!

Even if you are handy with tools, you may not have the time or inclination to get involved in the work on the house. I used to do all the carpentry, tiling and decorating myself. But as my portfolio grew I found I simply hadn't the time, so I delegated more and more to my contractors.

Unless you are a Corgi-registered plumber or a qualified, listed, electrician, don't even think about touching the gas appliances or electrics because you'll be breaking the law.

Finding good, reliable contractors is just about the best favour you can do yourself, but it takes time.

Rogue Traders

The first guy I employed to repair a roof for me was a complete charlatan who used substandard materials and made the roof worse than it was before he started. As soon as it rained, the water poured into the house. Having got his money, he wouldn't come back, despite the threat of legal action.

So I called in another roofer, who took me on to the roof and showed me all the mistakes the cowboy had made. Armed with photos and a statement from the new roofer, I took the first guy to court. He didn't contest it and so I was awarded judgment.

On this occasion I didn't get my money back or my court fees because the bailiffs reported that he was 'not known' at the address he had given. What many people don't realise is that even if the bailiffs go armed with a warrant and find the defendant at home, they have no power of entry and, unless they are invited in, cannot enter the property and seize goods. I have found that bailiffs usually give up after a couple of visits.

I've bumped into the rogue roofer a few times since and he just grins at me smugly. These people always know how to cheat the system.

I took another contractor to court who failed to return and replace some defective flashing over a kitchen extension. Yet again I got judgment but failed to get my money. This time, instead of bothering with bailiffs, I applied to the court for a 'garnishee' order against his bank account, which is a way of getting your money directly from the defendant's bank, provided you have the details of his account.

But the process is very slow, and by the time the garnishee order was activated, the account had been emptied, and you only get one go.

A guarantor I took to court for non-payment of his sister's rent did not respond to the court papers so judgment was awarded, but he wouldn't let the bailiffs into his flat. He shouted through the window to them that he wasn't the tenant's brother, and hadn't signed a guarantee. The bailiffs tried a few more times, but then advised me that this man was well known to them, and that I would never get money out of him.

So much for the small claims court. In these cases, and in others, I eventually had to give up, despite having obtained judgments, and having wasted money on court fees and many hours of filling in forms and writing court submissions. The Government really needs to look at the small claims process, and make it easier for a claimant to be paid what is owed.

Tom of all (well, most) Trades

But every cloud has a silver lining, and the guy who had put right the bad work done by the cowboy roofer turned out to be a godsend. Not only was he a good roofer, but he was also a carpenter by trade and ran his one-man business from home, with occasional help from his dad and seasonal hired labour.

Tom has now been with me for fifteen years. He does everything except gas and electrics and no job is too small or too dirty. He never charges call-out fees and doesn't seem to differentiate between weekends and weekdays. He will attend to anything and everything, from leaking cisterns, broken gates, cracked glass and leaning garden walls – and also takes on larger jobs like full extensions.

On one occasion, I bought a house where there had been rats in the loft. The local rodent officer had put down poison and now the dead furry bodies were rotting in the loft and there were flies everywhere.

Can you imagine climbing into a dark, hot, fly-blown loft and feeling around in the dusty fibreglass insulation for dead rats? I just couldn't face it so I asked Tom. He smiled his usual smile and said, "No problem". He didn't even charge me for it!

When I buy a new property, having cleared out the rubbish, I hand over the keys to Tom, who goes in and starts work without referring to me. He knows from previous experience what is needed to get the place ready for students. I used to employ a double-glazing firm to do my windows but they always subcontracted the fitting, and the results were never consistent.

Again, it was Tom who showed me evidence of their poor workmanship and said he could do the job better and cheaper – now Tom does all my windows too.

When I go on holiday I have no need to worry. I know that on my return, Tom will have attended to any and all emergencies and that he will charge a fair price for work genuinely done. Whenever I call him to ask him to do a job, no matter what time of day or night, his reply is always, "No problem".

So to what do I owe this loyalty and good service? First of all I count myself lucky to have found a guy who knows his stuff, never complains and makes excuses, and is always cheerful.

Keep Your Contractors Happy

But as with all my contractors, two things attract them to me: that I have a lot of properties so they know the work is regular, and that I always pay their bills by return of post. Treat others as you would be treated and you will get, and keep, good contractors.

So now I have a team of regular contractors on whom I can depend with confidence.

There is Raj the gas man, who does a full gas service and landlord's safety certificate for £45 and who, like Tom, will respond on the day I call him. How many plumbers will do that?

Then there's Jim the damp-course man, who always seems to be in pain and out of breath (maybe it's the chemicals!) but does a brilliant and thorough job for half the price of some of the big damp and timber-treatment companies. He sometimes even waives the bill in favour of my owing him a pint "sometime".

And there's Nathan, the gardener (with his ever-present Springer spaniel), who says he's got terrible financial problems. Yet he always has a ready smile and can do twenty gardens in two days at only £10 a garden.

Oleg is the carpet man, a bright young guy with film-star looks who, for as long as I've known him, has told me he wants to get into property, yet he is still on his knees fitting carpets, doing a whole house for £600.

Glen, who gets me vacuum cleaners and fridge-freezers, runs an Aladdin's-cave of a junk shop containing literally thousands of items, and always has that warm-hearted, avuncular approach to customers still found in the Midlands and the North.

My bed man is Abdul, who seems to genuinely care that my life should have purpose and be virtuous, and is always handing me free booklets and videos showing me the True Path to Happiness, as I hand him cash for the latest consignment of excellent beds.

And then there is Mr Grimshaw (some contractors prefer the old fashioned, dignified distance of retaining surnames with handles) who does all my locks and keys and never fails to wink when knocking 35% off the bill, "as it's you, sir". I bet he says that to all his customers!

And for the worst job of all, summer cleaning, I have Svetlana, a tall, beautiful, and very cheerful lady from Ukraine, with her sing-song high-pitched, heavily accented voice. She thinks nothing of working fifteen-hour shifts when there's a rush on, cleaning out the most disgusting smelly toilets and greasy kitchens, and is always ready again at eight the next morning.

You will gather that I am very fond of all these people. Personally, I regard them as the engine of the country's economy and a testament to the success of multicultural Britain. I feel privileged to count them among my business associates and friends. Without them, I couldn't run my business and my life would be duller. So find good contractors, treat them well and they will not only help your business to grow but they will also enhance the quality of your life.

Meeting the Right Standards

If you are embarking on a major renovation, you need to be aware of rules governing planning consent and building regulations. If your builder is any good he will advise you on these, but you can also get free advice from your local council.

It is always best to get advice before committing yourself to a property that needs building or planning consent because it might be refused. Sometimes, you may not even be aware that consent is needed, and could get caught out, just as I was on one occasion.

In 1997 I bought a former nursing home. It seemed an ideal student property, being only a mile from the university campus. It had nine extremely large double bedrooms, three bathrooms, two kitchens, an enormous sitting room and large separate dining room.

In addition to all that, it had a garage, off-road parking and an extensive, landscaped garden that the students loved. In those days, there were lots of groups of students wanting very large houses, and I had no trouble letting it to the first group of nine who came along.

House in Multiple Occupation (HMO)

But because it had been a nursing home, the local Council advised me that I would have to apply for planning permission to change its use into a house in multiple occupation (HMO) because there were more than six unrelated residents.

The number 'six' seemed to me to have been plucked from the air. At the same time, the housing department insisted that a property became an HMO when there were more than five unrelated residents and the Council tax department insisted the number was 'two or more'. And these departments were all part of the same local council!

But I assumed that getting the consent would be a formality. The house had all the required facilities and accommodation. It had a fire alarm system with linked smoke alarms in every room, emergency lighting on the staircases, self-closing fire doors everywhere, and had been well-maintained and regularly inspected while it was a nursing home. I couldn't believe that regulations affecting a shared house for students would be more severe than those for elderly and infirm residents, but I was wrong.

The problem arose with the concept of an HMO. The planning department seemed to view all HMOs as large buildings containing separate, self-contained bed-sits, with no communal areas, and tenanted by people who were not only unrelated, but who also led completely separate lives.

For that type of building, there are rules about providing places for off-road parking. Their response to my application for change of use was that I needed **fourteen** off-road parking spaces, because they viewed the nine bedrooms as nine separate family units, each requiring 1.5 parking spaces! Is that madness, or what?

I protested long and loud, explaining that these were students living, not separately, but as a family unit, sharing housekeeping etc. I said students rarely had cars (and certainly not 1.5 each!) and that most would walk or catch the bus to the university.

But the planning department was having none of it, claiming that although the present tenants were students, subsequent ones might not be. They said once change of use had been granted, there would be parking problems on the street if I did not provide sufficient off-road spaces. They did, however, agree to reduce the number of parking spaces to nine. It seems that rules can be bent but not waived!

So I took a long look at the garden and worked out how we could create nine spaces. There was room for two cars at the front, but to find seven more would require knocking down the garage and concreting half of the back garden. I wasn't too happy about doing this, but without the planning consent, I was told I could only use six of the nine bedrooms, so I submitted plans.

Then all hell broke loose because neighbours started objecting and, frankly, I didn't blame them. This was a very pleasant area with large family houses and big, mature gardens. Neighbours thought I was converting the house into bed-sits and that their gardens would be polluted by exhaust fumes and noise from the cars I was planning to park at the back of the house.

The case went to appeal. The most vociferous of the neighbours came, and told tales about another HMO up the road that was causing everyone endless grief, and two of my tenants came to support me, saying they lived as one family unit and only wanted peace and quiet.

But I lost, not because of the neighbours' objections but because it was decreed that my plans didn't allow sufficient turning area for the cars. Council officers had rushed off during the appeal, returning with computer print-outs of projected turning manoeuvres that, they claimed, "proved" that the cars wouldn't be able to turn around in the space provided. I was a beaten man, having spent very large sums on a specialist planning solicitor who assured me I would win.

For three more years I struggled on, putting only six tenants in a house that could easily accommodate nine. The simple maths of renting a property is that the first few rooms pay for all the overheads and the last few represent the profit. In a house of this size, by not renting three of the nine rooms, I was actually losing about 80% of my potential profit.

But I had the last laugh because, when I sold it after four years, the house went for three times the price I had paid for it, so I got my money back, and more. And the beautiful garden remains intact, no thanks to the council planners, who are supposed to be guardians of the environment.

So tread carefully if you are buying a property that may need consents, either planning or building. Adding a bathroom will certainly need consent, as will knocking down internal walls.

Sure, you can go ahead and do these things without anyone finding out (unless neighbours alert the local council). But when you come to sell the property, you will be required to produce evidence of the consents obtained and if you can't produce them, the sale will almost certainly fall through.

Assuming that your refurbishment does not need consents, there are still a number of rules governing what you do if you intend to let to students. Abiding by these will not only keep you on the right side of the law, but will also make the property more marketable.

Housing Acts

Space is too limited here to go into detail on all the rafts of housing legislation that have been implemented in recent years, but it is essential that you familiarise yourself with the sections of relevant legislation that relate to rental properties.

70

For example, shortly after I started letting, new regulations were introduced making it illegal to rent a property containing soft furnishings that presented a fire hazard. The only way of ascertaining whether the furniture complied was to check for labels. The problem was that, over previous years, there had been a growing awareness of the dangers of combustible furniture, with the result that many manufacturers had taken to putting on their own labels claiming that the furniture was 'fireproof', 'non-flammable', 'safe' etc.

When the new legislation came out, all these labels were dismissed as meaningless, and one, 'precise' definition became the only one acceptable, thus dismissing all others. In essence, all furniture manufactured in the UK since 1988 is supposed by law to comply with the regulations. But without the correct label, it is difficult to be certain when it was manufactured. NEVER put a piece of soft furnishing in your property unless it bears the label:

(a) CARELESSNESS CAUSES FIRE

(b) Batch/ID No DF 1234

To comply with the Furniture and Furnishings (Fire) (Safety) Regulations 1988

(c) This article does not include a Schedule 3 interliner

(d) All foams, fillings and composites have been tested to ensure compliance with the relevant ignability test. All covers and fillings have been tested to ensure that they are cigarette resistant. All covers have been tested to ensure that they are match resistant

And that's supposed to be 'precise'! Whichever bureaucratic android produced this convoluted pronouncement would no doubt be held up to ridicule by The Society for Plain English. But whether or not it makes sense, those are the words you need to find on the label under the cushions on your sofa, to be sure that it is legal.

Gas Appliances

Another recent piece of legislation concerned gas appliances, and was in reaction to deaths in rental properties from carbon monoxide poisoning. At the time of writing, the deaths of two children from carbon monoxide poisoning while on holiday in Greece is in the news and this underlines the importance to landlords of making sure that gas appliances are safe.

In the mid-Eighties, any plumber was allowed to install or repair gas appliances, but then along came the CORGI scheme, which required all plumbers working on gas to have undergone recent training, to have passed exams, and to be registered as a CORGI plumber. The CORGI scheme is extremely rigorous and closely monitored.

As a landlord, you are required by law to have all your gas appliances inspected by a registered CORGI plumber at least once a year and before the start of any new tenancy. Failure to do this is actually a criminal offence and you could be sent to prison for non-compliance. Besides that, do you really want to risk the lives of your tenants for want of spending a few pounds each year on a proper inspection?

Landlord Associations

To keep abreast of these regulations and to get advice on their implementation and a wide range of other matters relating to tenancies, the best thing you can do is to join a landlords association such as The Residential Landlords Association (www.rla.org.uk).

This excellent organisation publishes a monthly high-quality glossy magazine that is bursting with useful articles covering every aspect of buy-to-let and managing tenancies. It also holds a full programme of training events at both local and national level. The annual subscription is, of course, tax deductible!

Accreditation Schemes and Licensing

When I was starting out I was often aggrieved when prospective tenants tried to negotiate a rent reduction because they had friends living nearby who paid a lower rent. I knew the properties concerned, and also knew that the conditions and facilities offered were far inferior to mine.

I began to lobby the university, asking if they would inspect and recommend properties, to give the edge to those of us who aspired to higher standards. But they said they were under-resourced and that there was such a shortage of accommodation that they couldn't afford to turn landlords away. They were happy to let market forces work against the bad landlords.

The problem was that some students were so poor that they chose by necessity to live in squalid, damp and unsafe properties that were cheaper, and so standards just weren't rising. The Council's chairman of housing wrote a scathing article in the local newspaper, accusing all landlords of student houses of being 'Rachmans', and called for an improvement in standards.

At my protest of his tarring us all with the same brush, he wrote privately to me saying that I was the exception and that he knew my houses were excellent. Actually, he'd never heard of me before and had certainly never been inside any of my properties!

But armed with his letter from the paper, I went again to the university and suggested a ten-point benchmark scheme to which landlords could voluntarily subscribe. Eventually, the university called a meeting of local landlords and this, together with other ideas, was floated and was well received.

It appeared that other landlords had also been aggrieved at the comments in the newspaper and wanted to get rid of the cowboys who were undercutting prices.

So an accreditation scheme was discussed at a number of consultative meetings with landlords and was eventually introduced in 1998. At the same time, other similar schemes were being introduced in other parts of the country, and many other universities now have something similar in place.

The schemes are of two types: one is where the university asks for a landlord to supply gas and electrical certificates before they will advertise the properties. The other is a full inspection system, usually operated in conjunction with the local authority.

There was an assumption in the late Nineties on the part of some universities that the 'buy-to-let' bonanza would result in a surfeit of accommodation and that only those accredited would survive.

This assumption failed to take into account the fact that student numbers were also growing rapidly and so most landlords still had no problem finding tenants, whether or not they were accredited. But by not being accredited, they could not, of course use the universities facilities, publications and websites to advertise their properties, and had to rely, for the main part, on posters in windows, and word of mouth.

I submitted all my properties for accreditation, having done any necessary upgrades, and paid the joining fees (which also involved renewal fees every year and new inspections every three years).

In principle this all seemed like a very good idea but after a couple of years I came to realise that I was wasting my money. The scheme was poorly and inefficiently managed. This resulted in a long queue for inspections, and properties falling vacant for the forthcoming autumn were not being advertised until late spring or early summer.

In my experience, students start looking for the following year's accommodation as early as January and I am usually fully booked by late February.

I also found that the administrators of the scheme were high-handed and autocratic. Those doing the inspections often had absolutely no qualifications or experience in surveying but were just office staff with tick-sheets on clipboards.

In consequence, many did not know what they were looking for or looking at. I have been into newly accredited properties that were actually unfit for human habitation but had been passed for students to live in. I once went to view a house for sale, and the owner proudly showed me his new accreditation certificate.

Going around with her clipboard the week before, the inspector had failed to notice that many of the electrical sockets were not actually connected to the mains. She had not noticed that there was dry rot in the cellar, one of the outside drains had collapsed and was causing subsidence to the corner of the house and one of the bedrooms was so small there wasn't room to swing a proverb, let alone a cat.

At the other extreme, some of the inspectors were demanding improvements to properties that were simply not necessary. One demanded I replace a boarded-up window on a locked outhouse because it was showing signs of rot, even though the tenants never had cause to use it. He also insisted that I replace a fire door in a bedroom because the tenant had pierced it with a single drawing pin, thus "compromising its integrity". I joke not. How dare he suggest that one of my doors might be dishonest!

I stuck a pin-head of wood filler in the microscopic hole and called him back to inspect the 'new' door, which he duly passed as safe!

Getting Personal

In some cases, those running the accreditation schemes were making personal judgments about a landlord's suitability, even though such matters were not part of the scheme. One local landlord had a minor brush with the law, the outcome of which was luridly and inaccurately reported in the local tabloid press, complete with all the embellishments of a meaty scandal.

The incident concerned was a personal tragedy and had absolutely nothing to do with his tenants, his financial probity or his ability to carry out his responsibilities as a landlord. Yet when a copy of this press report reached the university, he received a letter saying that it would no longer advertise his properties or have anything more to do with him.

He wrote in to appeal but was not even granted a hearing, the decision-makers hiding behind their closed doors, refusing to comment further. With his only source of advertising removed overnight, this man faced financial ruin because his business depended entirely on students from the local university being his tenants, having set up all his properties for that purpose.

At the very time in his life when he needed the most support, the university chose to cut the feet from under him. But he was determined and resourceful, and found other ways of marketing his properties to students, circumventing the university and the accreditation scheme. He rose to become the biggest landlord of student properties in the region and became a thorn in the side of the university.

What bothers me about the new licensing scheme is that landlords can be turned away not only on the quality of their properties but also on whether they are 'fit and proper persons' to be landlords. It currently only affects properties with five or more tenants and three or more storeys but is widely expected to be extended to include all student properties in some areas.

This seems to me to be yet another example of institutional prejudice against landlords. Why should landlords have to be judged 'fit and proper' persons to run a small business that, in the case of student houses, means all their customers are adults who are fully protected by the law anyway?

Why not shopkeepers, plumbers or electricians? And what about those who run businesses where contact with customers is of a more intimate nature, like photographers, directors of model agencies, private dance teachers and so on?

My contention is that unless a landlord has a court order specifying that, because of previous misdemeanours (like flouting gas regulations or withholding deposits), he must not work as a landlord, then that should be the only criterion upon which 'fit and proper' should be determined. And such judgments should be not be made by faceless bureaucrats behind closed doors.

The other side of the coin is, of course, that many tenants are not 'fit and proper' and yet no one is suggesting there are categories of people who should never be allowed to rent a house.

Tenancy Agreement

A more reasonable way of dealing with the issue of suitability is to have a tenancy agreement that obliges both sides to adhere to an agreed code of conduct. The very first condition my tenants and I agree to is "to maintain a courteous and considerate approach to one another".

That seems to me to be fundamental to an arrangement whereby someone is living in a house I own, which I want them to look after and pay their rent and, in return, they expect me to provide suitable accommodation and a responsive service.

If all tenancy agreements contained this clause, and others like it that define levels of service and conduct from both parties, then the issue of a person being 'fit and proper' would be covered by the agreement and would legally enforceable.

In any case, there are already plenty of laws in place to protect tenants although some would argue that there are not enough to protect landlords.

On one occasion I actually evicted a female tenant because she failed to be 'courteous and considerate'. She took the view that landlords only respond when shouted at and, after three months of late-night abusive phone calls and adversarial confrontations, I wrote to her and to her guarantor warning her of breach of contract.

Her behaviour didn't improve so I served her with an eviction notice, which she didn't contest, and she left a month later. Had she refused to leave, I would have had great difficulty (and incurred much expense) in enforcing the eviction.

One can only hope that when landlords apply to have their properties licensed, decisions made about their suitability will be transparent and that there will be a proper appeals system.

Going it Alone

After a couple of years of paying very high fees, and being frustrated by the inefficient way in which my local accreditation scheme was being administered, I decided to go it alone. Clearly, I would be competing with other landlords who were accredited, so it was essential that my properties not only met the standards in the accreditation scheme but exceeded it.

Most accreditation schemes have similar criteria, so before you embark on your renovations, make sure you know what they are. It is very expensive and disruptive to go back into a property to add extra electrical sockets etc when you have laid carpets, furnished and have tenants in situ.

If there is an accreditation scheme in your area, it may look something like this:

- **Repairs**
  The property should be in a generally good state of repair and should conform to regulations regarding size and space for living accommodation, adequate window-opening space for escape, adequate ventilation, and so on. If in doubt about this, check with the housing department of your local council and also with the local fire department, who will provide free advice.

- **Amenities**
  There should be at least one bathroom and one kitchen per five tenants, and these should be in a clean and serviceable condition. The kitchen must have adequate storage for food and crockery, including a good-sized fridge-freezer, and wipeable working surfaces. Cookers must have a working surface on either side of the hob. There should be a communal sitting room with adequate seating for all tenants. Bedrooms must be big enough for a bed, adequate storage of clothes and have ample space for the student to study.

- **Notice board**
  There should be a notice board in a communal area containing the following information: gas and electrical certificates, procedure in the event of a fire, the landlord's address or contact details, an inventory of the contents in the property, and other such notices regarding the management of the tenancies.

- **Gas safety**
  All gas appliances must be checked and certificated by a Corgi-registered plumber at least once a year and at any change of tenancy. This is a legal requirement and you will have to send in your certificate to the accrediting office and also display a valid certificate in the property. **Warning: you can be sent to prison for not doing this!**

- **Electrical Safety**
  All electrical circuits in the property should be tested and certificated with a 'periodic report' every three years

(some schemes reduce that to five years and others accept that a full re-wire need not be inspected for ten years).

In addition, all portable electrical items should be inspected and given PAT certificates annually. Any electrical work carried out since January 1, 2005 should have been done by an electrician with an 'EAS' certificate of competence, or one who is registered with the local authority. This initiative is intended to bring electrical safety into line with gas safety

All bedrooms and sitting rooms should have two double electrical sockets, and kitchens should have three double sockets.

There should be smoke alarms on landings, stairwells, and in hallways. Where there is a feature on the ceiling that impedes the flow of smoke across the ceiling, the smoke alarms should be placed on both sides of the impeding feature.

There should also be a heat sensor on the kitchen ceiling. All smoke alarms, and the heat sensor, should be run off the mains, and be interlinked so that when one is set off, the others are also activated. They should also contain rechargeable batteries that are trickle-fed from the mains, so that, in the event of a power cut, the alarm system still works.

- **Fire safety**
  All soft furnishings should bear the label described earlier, and there should also be a fire blanket in close proximity to the cooker.

- **Locks**
  All locks on doors should be capable of being opened from the inside without the use of a key (so that in an emergency, escape in the dark is possible).

- **Ventilation**
  Bathrooms and kitchens must contain extractor fans with humidistat controls so that they are activated as soon as humidity levels rise.

HMO Licensing

Under the Housing Act 2004, any rental property with five or more unrelated tenants AND three or more storeys MUST be licensed with the local authority, and failure to do so, or any breaches of the licence, could result in a criminal prosecution.

The criteria for registering a property are very similar to those in the accreditation scheme above. However, the fire precautions will be much more rigorous, and may necessitate fire doors on all rooms, interlinked fire and smoke alarms in all rooms, fire-proofed walls on upper staircases, an emergency lighting system, fire escape route notices, and strategically placed fire extinguishers.

You may also be required to install a sprinkler system, but since each property is different in construction and layout, it is best to seek the advice of your local fire department, which is free. It is not surprising that many landlords are choosing to get rid of their HMO properties and, in some areas, this is already resulting in a shortage of private accommodation for students.

Returnable Deposits

Included in the Act is a scheme for tenants' deposits. It is intended to protect tenants from landlords who over-charge or withhold deposits unfairly, and landlords from tenants who abscond without paying the final month's rent (although it is unclear how the latter will be achieved).

The new scheme will come into effect in the spring of 2007 in England and Wales, but is still under discussion for Scotland and Northern Ireland. Landlords will have a choice of two schemes, the first being to lodge the deposit with the Tenancy Deposit Scheme (TDP), which they must do within two weeks of taking the deposit.

The second is to retain the deposit but to take out insurance that guarantees to the tenant that the deposit will be returned. Provided one or the other scheme is used, there will be no need to refer disputes to the courts, the idea being that the scheme will be able to fund dispute resolution. It remains to be seen, however, whether the volume of disputes can be handled by the scheme.

Other Features in Your Property

In both the accreditation scheme and the HMO licensing, the main focus is on safety, which should rightly be the priority. But if you want to make your property more marketable, it's a good idea to go for even higher standards and make those points a highlight in your marketing.

As a matter of policy I always put in more electrical sockets than the minimum. This costs very little when you are having a full rewire done. It also reduces the number of trailing cables that your tenants will need to power the increasing number of electrical items students have these days.

I also always put self-closing fire doors on kitchens, even though none of my properties are licensed HMOs. Again, these are not too expensive and will not only save lives but may also limit damage to your property in the event of a fire. Most fires start in kitchens.

I do not put washing machines into kitchens because these are items most likely to break down through overuse or misuse, and I don't relish being called out to a flooded kitchen on a Sunday evening because someone's sock is stuck in the waste pipe.

Instead, I put in the plumbing for automatic washing machines and advise the tenants where they can buy or hire one locally. One local shop supplies reconditioned washing machines for about £50 with a six-month guarantee – very little when split between all tenants and saves me a lot of hassle.

Some landlords I know put in washing machines but then tell the tenants that they are responsible for beak-downs. Legally, that won't wash! Anything owned by you in a property is your responsibility.

For the same reason, I don't put in microwave ovens because tenants damage them too easily by putting in metal objects. While I want to provide good quality accommodation, at the same time I want to reduce the amount of work and number of call-outs I am likely to get from misuse of electrical items.

In bathrooms I always put in both a bath and a shower (which is electrically operated and independent of the boiler, so that there is still hot water for showering in the event of the boiler failing).

Where there is room, I make the shower separate from the bath. The ideal is two rooms – one with a shower and lavatory and the other with a bath and lavatory.

If you are lucky enough to buy a property with sinks in bedrooms, so much the better, because students love that, of course.

Years ago I used to go to the expense of have a landline installed at all of my properties so that I could contact the tenants and they could contact their parents. It was a good marketing ploy but it was very expensive because, at the time, and we're talking ten or more years ago, BT charged around £100 each time to install a line.

Now, of course, all students have mobile phones so don't need landlines as a basic necessity. But what they do need, instead, is access to the internet. In urban areas, most properties have cable running past the front door, so it is a relatively simple matter to get the relevant company to run the service into the property.

You can choose to let the tenants arrange this themselves or, to make your property much more attractive, provide a 'wireless' internet facility as standard and included in the rent. Given that a growing number of students have PCs and laptops that can pick up wireless signals, this will make the property extremely attractive, providing not only internet access, but also a phone line and TV channels.

Ventilation

Ventilation in bedrooms is sometimes a problem and it's difficult to tell before the tenants move in where the problems might occur. Where the room is not properly ventilated, water vapour from the students' breath or drying clothes will gather on cold, external walls, especially behind beds and wardrobes and result in the accumulation of black mould.

While this can easily be removed with a solution of washing-up liquid and bleach, it will be necessary to address its cause. Two things reduce condensation: warmth and ventilation. Where this cannot be improved by simply turning up the heating and opening the windows, it will be necessary to install vents in an external wall, one high and one low, so that a current of air can flow from one to the other.

Nothing must impede this flow if it is to work effectively. The trouble is that many students stuff socks or paper into the vents to stop the draft, so you are then back to square one; but at least you've done what you could!

Security

Some accreditation schemes also require security measures to be in place to deter burglars.

In my experience, most determined burglars will enter a house regardless of what measures are in place, but clearly there are some who will be deterred if you take a few precautions.

I am not a big fan of burglar alarms because they can only be activated when the property is empty and a burglar will usually have finished his work and gone before neighbours respond. Alarms also have a nasty habit of going off by themselves in midsummer when the students are away. This results in very angry neighbours ringing the landlord to complain about alarms that have been ringing all night.

A landlord I know had his property broken into by the police to stop a bell ringing, and had to pay himself for the damage they caused. A better deterrent is to have security lights at the back of the property that are motion-activated and will expose someone trying to gain entry.

Obviously you also need to ensure that your external doors are protected with good quality locks. Your insurance company will certainly recommend a minimum standard, but your accreditation scheme may limit the number of bolts you are allowed to have on the inside of external doors.

It goes without saying that the police are not big fans of accreditation schemes! If your property has glazed panels in the front door, or on either side of it, you need to take measures to ensure that a burglar cannot break those and reach in to open the door from the inside. A simple measure is to fix a piece of sturdy wire netting over the glazed panels. This prevents someone reaching in, but still allows light into the hallway.

Decorating

I always decorate in white or magnolia because it is light, bright, and very easy to match when touching up marks on the walls after the annual cleaning. I insist that tenants never paint walls themselves and charge them heavily if they do so, reminding them that the next tenant may not be partial to their choice of purple with black stars, and so they will have to pay for the room to be returned to magnolia.

In any case, a light colour provides a much better background for the various posters that the tenant will wish to put up, and for this, I tell them Blu-tac is OK, but not pins. My carpet man puts down cord carpet for me which, although difficult to vacuum, is cheap to lay and reasonably hard wearing.

More recently, I have started installing laminate floors (with a few scatter rugs to break up the hard surface) which cost only a little more than fitted carpets, but which will last for many years, and make cleaning so much easier.

Furnishing

As previously mentioned, I try always to provide bedrooms that are big enough for double beds.

An early mistake I made was to think that while it was OK to provide second-hand tables and chairs, a bed, being such a personal item, needed to be new, or as new as possible, so I went out and spent around £200 each on double beds.

The problem with beds of that price is that, for all their pretty fabric covering, the bases are actually made of thin cardboard stretched across scrap pine that was probably rejected by a match factory.

When the tenant returns home from a good Friday night out and slumps carelessly on to the bed, the bed base collapses.

And my idea of clean fresh mattresses didn't take account of the fact that no bed remains fresh after a year of leaking body fluids. (Apologies to more squeamish readers but this is a fact of life if you're a landlord).

So what is the answer?

Enter Abdul, my streetwise bed man, who knows a man, who knows another man, who gets top quality two-year-old trampoline-strength beds (including waterproof mattress covers) from hotels doing refurbishments, "only fifty quid to you, my friend, cos I like your face, innit".

The moral of this story is: don't waste money on new beds, find yourself someone like Abdul.

The same is true of three-piece suites. These, more than any other item in a student house take the hardest wear, and rarely last more than two years, so why buy new when a clean and very serviceable suite can be bought for £75 in your local free-ads newspaper (and transported in your trailer!).

What Furnishings Students Want

For a student, the bedroom is much more than just a place to sleep. Although the bed may be a basic requirement, much more is needed to make it into a comfortable, functional room that is also a study, escape, a place for private expression of personality and, dare I say it, a love nest.

The student will take care of the personality side of things with lurid posters, drapes and items that glow in the dark.

Your side of the bargain should be to provide a desk with a chair, a wardrobe or hanging rail (many students prefer these), cupboards and/or chests of drawers for clothes storage.

Also provide shelving for books and ornaments, an easy chair if there is enough floor space, curtains (with nets for overlooked rooms), a mirror, bin, and a light shade.

As well as the three-piece suite, the sitting room needs a coffee table (which discourages but doesn't prevent, glasses and cups from being put on the floor!) and a table or stand on which to put their TV and DVD player (which they supply!).

The under-stairs cupboard will contain an ironing board and cleaning materials, including a mop and bucket, vacuum cleaner, dustpan and brush, etc.

Most students bring a lot of kitchen utensils but, as well as a cooker and large half-and-half fridge-freezer, I always put in basic kit. It includes a saucepan set, baking tins and dishes, bowls and measuring jugs, cooking utensils, a kettle, teapot, trays, and a good supply of crockery, cutlery, and glasses – usually two of everything for each person.

This is one area where I make net gains each year. While I have to replace beds and settees, I always end up with far more kitchen utensils than I started with and now have a garage full of spares.

Incidentally, regarding storage, it pays to buy a property with a garage once your portfolio is getting big enough to have the need for somewhere to store things.

Some years ago a church sold me a very large house that was converted into two flats. It had a triple, hangar-sized garage, which has proved ideal for storing my trailer and all my spare furniture, thus freeing-up my garage at home!

The bathroom should contain a good mirror and shelving or cupboards adequate for storage of bathroom items, including racks above the sink and in the shower. There is nothing worse than seeing a bath with forty-seven bottles of shampoo perched precariously along the edge for want of shelving.

Tony's Tips

- Anticipate the worst when you first take possession of a property.

- Make sure that any work you do makes the property more sellable.

- Buy a van and trailer.

- Always pay your contractors' bills promptly and they will give you priority service.

- Check whether consents are needed before you buy a property.

- When buying soft furnishing, always look for the right label.

- Join the RLA or other landlord organization for on-going help and advice.

- Whether or not you choose to join the local accreditation scheme, make sure that your properties match or exceed its standards.

- Decorate in white or magnolia – it's easier to touch up.

- Don't waste money on new furniture – it doesn't stay new for long.

- Get a garage for storage!

Chapter 7

Finding Tenants – The Most Important Job of All

Accreditation

If you decide to register with your local accreditation scheme (provided there is a local scheme) and have your properties inspected, the deal is that the fee you pay covers the cost of the inspection and the listing of your property on the website and in the sheets distributed to prospective tenants.

I have received very different reports of how well this works from various parts of the country and it very much seems to depend on how clued-up the individuals are in the accommodation office you are dealing with.

But no matter how efficient the accommodation office is, bear in mind that they have their own agendas and priorities and their first loyalty is to the university and the students, not to private landlords. It matters not a jot to them whether you find tenants, so unless a particular individual in the accommodation office owes you a favour or is a personal friend, do not just sit back and expect them to fill your houses.

The only real advantage of being accredited is to be able to reassure your tenants and their parents that your properties have reached a certain standard. But it seems a high price to pay what with having to pay fees annually or biannually and having to chase them to ask why your properties haven't been advertised. Also, why the adverts continue to contain mistakes, given all the forms you've had to fill in and the cheques you've had to sign.

Doing Your Own Marketing

My own experience convinced me that I had to take matters into my own hands and do all my own marketing so that I had control of the deadlines and could get to the prospective tenants first. And I soon found that not only was it easy but it was cheap and I have saved thousands of pounds by choosing not to use the local accreditation scheme.

Of course, the first hurdle I had to face was the fact that the university actually tried to operate a closed shop by warning students not to rent properties that were not accredited and to avoid, for example, properties advertised in local windows.

But students are not stupid, are quite capable of making up their own minds about the suitability of a property and really don't need to be told what to do by the university.

Consequently, I've never had problems letting properties despite operating outside the accreditation scheme, simply because my properties achieve higher standards than those described in the scheme – and my prices are competitive.

Get Yourself a Website

When planning my marketing strategy, the first thing I did was to construct a website. Well, not me personally, being of that Luddite generation that still can't operate video recorders (remember those?) and think that soft toilet paper is an extravagance.

But that year I had a tenant doing a degree in web design and, having ascertained that it had nothing to do with arachnids, I asked him to create my first website in exchange for a couple of rent-free weeks.

I can't claim, of course, that it scored many search engine hits but it achieved two other things.

It gave my business a degree of professionalism and provided a point of reference on leaflets I gave out so that students could look up my properties, see photos, and read full details before viewing.

It also served to reassure parents who don't read the details of accreditation schemes but were glad to look at my website and see that little Johnny was moving into a house with a number of listed safety features, and was well-furnished.

That first website has been re-done several times over as I have added more and more properties to the portfolio but it has never cost me more than a hundred pounds to create and upload, having always used tenants or friends to do the work.

Now it is quite sophisticated, easy to navigate and full of relevant information. The opening page contains a simple map of the city showing the location of the university sites and the proximity of all my properties. By clicking on a particular property on the map, another page opens showing a photo and giving full details of that property – its location, size, accommodation, and so on.

Other pages on the website refer to relevant safety legislation, the local accreditation scheme, and go on to list all the safety features in my properties. Prospective tenants or parents are invited to inspect. Actually, the site is obviously so reassuring to parents that in the ten years since I have had it, only one parent has ever asked for an inspection prior to the tenant moving in.

The website also has a contact page, encouraging email and telephone enquiries. The final page contains testimonials – selected extracts from letters I have received over the years from tenants or parents, all of which make good reading.

The Taxcafe team has created a sample student site which you will find at www.topdigs4u.co.uk. Having a website like this set up shouldn't cost more than a couple of hundred pounds in web design fees and will cost you about £30 per year in web hosting fees.

Doing the Footwork

So, with my website in place, but not being confident students would find it using search engines, my next strategy was to find them instead. The university took the view that students don't start looking for accommodation for the new academic year until well after Easter. Their inspection and advertising cycle was based on that premise and details of properties for the autumn rarely appeared before May.

I have heard similar stories from many other parts of the country. The reality, of course, is that students move into hall in the autumn of their first year and, within weeks have formed new friendships and start talking about finding a flat or house for the second year.

By Christmas or early January that talk translates into action and they actually start looking for somewhere, and that's where I step in. Each January, I run off a few hundred fliers and spend a couple of hours walking around the halls of residence dropping them into letterboxes and pigeon-holes. Even before I get home, my phone is ringing and appointments to view are going into my diary.

Fixing Rents

Before you start your viewings you need to decide on your rent levels. If you are providing top quality accommodation, then there is every justification for charging top rents.

Many students will actually be guided to your properties by the rents you charge, and therefore come with certain expectations. The story goes that when BMW launched one of its models in the 1970s it failed to sell, so they doubled the price and it sold like hot cakes.

Certainly, if you are targeting potential tenants very early in the year, you can hope to get higher rents but if you still have properties unfilled by the summer, then you may have to drop your prices.

The rents you charge will be governed by both the location of the property and by the size of the rooms – the further from the university and the smaller the room, the lower the price.

Sometimes you will get couples who wish to co-habit and, provided the house is big enough and the other tenants don't mind, you can earn a little more from a room by charging a higher price for a couple sharing. In the year of writing, I have four co-habiting couples of various sexual persuasions.

As the years go by, you will get a better idea about which of your properties can realise the best rent. Those that consistently prove hard to let should be sold and replaced with others that are better located or have better accommodation.

Conducting Viewings

A lot of time can be wasted waiting for prospective tenants to arrive at a property at the appointed hour, and many don't make it at all.

This is where my van comes in handy. Rather than meeting them at the property, I always arrange to collect them from hall. They really like and appreciate the gesture, and I am certain it goes a long way to establishing a good relationship with them. And by collecting them and returning them afterwards, it is possible, of course, to see several properties in one session, thus giving them a choice, which they also appreciate.

En route, I talk about the properties and the tenancy arrangements so they know what to expect. After the viewings, I always warn them that an early decision is vital if they are not to lose the property of their choice, because I have so many people doing viewings at that particular time, which in January and February is usually true.

I tell them to go off and think about it, to check the website, talk to their parents and ring back with any questions. Invariably, those who are keen will make a decision before the end of the day and call me back to say they want a particular house.

Sort Out the Legals

Next, I run off two tenancy agreements and a rent guarantee form each, and hand-deliver the package to one of the group taking the house.

The package also contains a letter asking for everything to be completed, signed and returned within two weeks, during which time I promise not to show that property to anyone else.

As well as asking for the paperwork, I also insist on the returnable deposits in full to secure the tenancy.

I show more flexibility about asking for the summer retainer, recognising that to demand this at the same time may be asking too much, so we usually agree a later date for the retainer to be handed over.

Once all tenancy agreements, rent guarantees and deposits are in, I write confirming that the house is theirs, and by having started my letting cycle well before most other landlords, I am usually fully let by the end of February.

I occasionally do another leaflet drop in February and, if a group withdraws later, or if I have a new house coming on line, then I might do a third drop, but that is really the only advertising I do that involves any effort from me.

Much to the annoyance of the university, I was one of those landlords who put up notices in windows. They always worked quite well but a few years ago I went one better and had large, colourful, plastic-laminated signs made, and screwed one on the front of all my properties to attract passing trade.

I had noticed similar signs put up by universities in other student cities to identify registered student houses. I decided that if they could do it, so could I.

The trouble is, it's actually against the planning regulations to have such a sign on permanent display – it is only permissible when there is actually a vacancy at the property where the sign is displayed.

But the reality is that the local council will only make you take them down when someone complains, as happened with one of mine. But the others have remained in position, and no one seems to mind.

The number of calls I get as a result of people seeing these signs (which contain my phone number and my website address), is phenomenal and certainly well worth the £80 or so they cost to produce.

The other marketing strategy, into which I have no input, is word of mouth. If you provide good-quality houses and an efficient, responsive service for your tenants, word gets around, and my tenants kindly recommend me to their friends.

Nothing beats a personal recommendation. There have been occasions when houses have been passed from one generation of students to another for several years running, with no input from me at all.

In one case, I have a house where I have not had to conduct viewings for nine years.

__Tony's Tips__

- Do your own marketing – don't rely on the university to find your tenants.

- Start letting your properties in January for the following autumn.

- Construct a website.

- Collect and take students to viewings.

Chapter 8

Managing Your Tenancies

Moving the Tenants in

Your first batch of tenants will most likely move into your new property either in June or September. Years ago very few students stayed over the summer but now that there is an imperative on almost all of them to earn money, increasing numbers choose to stay in their university towns where there may be more chance of a job than back home.

Nearly half of all my tenants now stay for the summer. This is good news for landlords of course because, instead of just a 40-44 week tenancy with a summer retainer, you can count on some tenants wishing to sign up for 52 weeks.

The Notice Board

In your final touches to the property before tenants move in, make sure that all necessary notices are posted on the notice board. These will include the inventory of house contents, contact details for you (required under most accreditation schemes), and escape procedure in the event of a fire. Add any other notices that you feel may reduce the number of phone calls you receive from tenants within the first few days of moving in.

You need to bear in mind that, other than their year in hall, many tenants will not have lived independently before, and some hand-holding may be necessary at first, but you can anticipate most of the likely questions in advance, by putting up notices bearing the answers.

Over the years, I have produced so many notices that it all became too much for the notice board, so I combined many of them into one document that I called 'Getting the most from you tenancy' (see Appendix B).

I email this to all new tenants after they have signed tenancy agreements, and also post it on notice boards. This answers most questions before they are asked.

The First Arrival

You will need to meet the first tenant at the property to let them in. If you leave a set of keys in each room, the first one can let in the others when they arrive, thus saving you the trouble.

When the first one arrives, it's also best to read the meters with him or her. Even though gas and electricity are their responsibility, not yours, it's a good idea to keep your own record of the start readings just in case there are any disputes later. Make it clear to the tenant that it is their responsibility to register with the suppliers and to submit the start readings.

I choose not to have pre-payment meters in my properties because it is always such a hassle to get tokens or cards during periods between tenancies when I need power in the properties for cleaning. In any case, power from post-payment meters is cheaper, and I mention that when showing tenants around, which pleases them, of course.

It's a good idea to get the first tenant who arrives to check the inventory and to sign a copy while you are there, and then there can be no dispute at a later date regarding the contents or condition of the property.

As I always spend a great deal of time and effort getting my properties ready, I am always pleased when parents accompany the first tenants moving in, and enjoy the positive feedback they give on the quality of the accommodation.

Interestingly, I have never had a complaint about accommodation at the stage of moving in although some have tried to claim when moving out that the house was dirty or poorly maintained at the start. This was an excuse for the condition in which they were leaving it, to which my response has always been – "Well, why didn't you say so at the time?" There's no answer to that.

In a new house, with a new set of tenants, there are invariably a few minor teething problems, but once those are out of the way the tenants usually settle down and you hear nothing from them. The next job, of course, is to collect the rent.

Collecting Rent

Years ago I foolishly went to collect rent once a month in person. More often than not I came away empty handed, or with only some of the rent, plus a long list of things in the house that needed my attention.

I was making a rod for my own back. I learned the hard way that the onus should be on the tenant to send the rent and not on the landlord to collect it. So now my tenancy agreements make it quite clear that it is the tenant's responsibility to get the rent to me by the deadline.

I allow rent to be paid either termly, to coincide with the arrival of loans, or monthly by standing order, and those opting for the latter are given a pro-forma to send to their bank. To check that these come in on time, I use internet banking to look at my account at regular intervals. I discourage monthly payments by cheque simply because of the extra work involved on my part in chasing it and banking it.

Dealing with Slow Payers

As mentioned previously, I try to be flexible with those tenants whose finance is not in place by rent days. I will always agree to a deferment or to receive post-dated cheques by those who contact me first to discuss it.

But inevitably, there is always a minority who fail to pay on time, and who don't bother to contact me. I always let it run for a few days before sending out my first reminders. This is usually a note enclosed with receipts of those who have paid, telling those who haven't to do so as soon as possible, or to call me.

For most, this is enough, and a cheque or phone call follows. Those who continue to ignore me then get a text message or an email, and this is repeated every few days. After a couple of weeks, I then call the rent guarantors.

My call is always very polite and charming, simply telling them that Johnny has forgotten to pay his rent, is not responding to my calls or messages and asking if they would kindly sort it out.

In almost all cases, this does the trick, and it is extremely rare not to get the rent after that. Where it does happen, I then write formally to the guarantor asking if, as guarantor, they would now please pay the rent, which is X weeks overdue.

Threat of Eviction

In the most extreme cases I then write threatening eviction and court action. I point out to the guarantor that a county court judgment affects credit history and the ability to get loans, and that bailiffs always take goods to up to ten times the value of the debt to be sure to cover all costs.

On my part, this is very much a bluff because I really don't want to evict tenants once the academic year is under way. It's always hard at that stage to find replacements, and even when a county court judgment is awarded, there is no guarantee I'll get my money back.

To date, I have never actually evicted a tenant for non-payment of rent, simply because no one has ever called my bluff. One way or another, they all pay up. It's usually better to let a non-payer stay until the end of the tenancy, and then take the guarantor to court for the whole amount, rather than evict the tenant mid-way through the year, and have to try to find a replacement.

Once the rent has been paid, I leave it at that, but I make a note of the date payment is received so that if the same tenant is persistently late every time throughout the tenancy period, I feel justified in making extra charges.

There are two ways of doing this. One is to charge for the letters and phone calls you have to make to get the rent and which may require a lot of evidence to justify the charge if challenged. The other is to charge a flat rate for the number of days late.

Whichever system you use, it must be clearly described in your tenancy agreement. In mine, it states that I will charge £1 per day for each day the rent is late. In most case, I waive this charge, but where the tenant is persistently late, I make the charge in the form of a deduction from the deposit at the end.

One parent complained that this was unfair and exorbitant and asked the Students Union to refer my charges to the Office of Fair Trading. My defence of the charge was that it was actually less than some letting agents would charge in similar circumstances where, for each reminder letter, they would be charging in the region of £30. The Office of Fair Trading agreed with me, and ruled that my charge was fair.

Keep a Record of Payments

It is very important that you carefully record all rent payments so that, if there is any dispute over whether a payment has been made, you are able to be certain in your response.

Payments directly into your bank account are the easiest to verify but payments by cheque or in cash need careful recording. I maintain an overview sheet for each property, showing names, dates, amounts due, and amounts paid. I also issue written receipts from a simple duplicate receipt book for each payment made.

When paying in cheques to my bank, I also record the name and property against each cheque on the paying-in slip. Thus I have three separate recordings of each cheque received. If a cheque 'bounces' I contact the tenant and ask for another, with £5 added for the inconvenience it causes me – this charge is also enshrined in the tenancy agreement. If it bounces a second time, then I ask for a cash payment.

Beside student loans, there are other emergency funds available to students who are suffering particular hardships, and I have sometimes liaised with the Students Union in these cases. I am always willing to work with these people and show that I can be flexible and reasonable if approached properly.

In exceptional circumstances this has sometimes resulted in my agreeing to extend rent payments beyond a tenancy period, or to agree to weekly payments, just so long as I can be assured that payments will eventually be made. It really is a question of judging each case on its merits.

I recently had a tenant who was injured in a fight, missed a lot of his lectures, and so temporarily left his course to repeat the year. As a result, he didn't receive the final instalment of his loan and was unable to pay rent for the last eight weeks of his tenancy.

His mother was his guarantor but she was out of work, and so he promised to work all summer and pay me the rent owing by the autumn. I had the choice of getting a court order to make sure he did, or take him on trust. In this case, I trusted him, and he paid, albeit slightly later than he promised, thus saving me a lot of hassle with the courts.

So, although a degree of vigilance is essential, it should be tempered with reason, if you wish to collect all your rent. No matter how late a tenant may be with rent, I always maintain a polite and friendly manner, showing understanding, sympathy, and fairness, but always underpinned with firmness.

I never allow my tenants to confuse my kindness with weakness. As mentioned earlier, my collection rate is well over 99%.

Tenancy Withdrawals

One problem that you may encounter at the beginning of the tenancy, or perhaps half way through the year, is that of a tenant who withdraws from the university and therefore from the tenancy.

Thankfully, this is a rare event and it invariably happens at a time when the academic year is already under way and all students already have accommodation, so it is extremely difficult to find replacements.

To cover myself against such an eventuality, I insist that my tenants always sign up for the full academic year, and that where they withdraw prematurely, they remain responsible for meeting rent deadlines until a replacement tenant can be found.

I make it clear that it's their responsibility to find a replacement although obviously I also put out feelers too. When the replacement is found, I refund any over-payment of rent by the outgoing tenant, but make a small charge for the extra work involved in doing viewings, issuing new tenancy agreements, and so on.

Most tenants understand their position on this very well, and matters are usually resolved amicably, and without loss of rent.

Serving Notice

To comply strictly with the legislation affecting assured short-hold tenancies, you are supposed to issue notices to quit soon after the tenants move in. This is called a 'Section 21' notice, and it tells the tenants what they already know from their tenancy agreement – that they are required to vacate the property by the final date on that agreement.

It seems like doubling up to have to issue such a notice, but a judge will not grant you an eviction order at the end of the tenancy unless you have served the notice both at the beginning of the tenancy and again, two months from the end.

It's up to you whether you really wish to go through with this rigmarole. I don't actually, the reason being that, in my experience, students never overstay their welcome and, when their courses end, they leave like lambs.

It's obviously a different matter if you wish to evict them mid-term for some misdemeanour. In that case, it is essential to use the appropriate forms and to cite the correct grounds for eviction, otherwise, should the matter go to court, you will be ruled out of order, and have to start proceedings all over again.

Responding to Problems

Provided you keep on top of your maintenance jobs and do thorough checks of everything between tenancies, the number of call-outs you get will be minimal, but do expect some.

In fact, I get rather worried about the tenants who never call me out because I would rather have a minor problem reported before it becomes major.

One such problem occurred a few years ago where a blocked gutter was causing damp to enter a bedroom ceiling. The young man occupying the room seemed oblivious to the large damp patch slowly crawling down his bedroom wall, turning black with mould as it did so.

He liked to keep the curtains shut and mould loves darkness, so after nine months, the mould had become full-size fungi and had eaten into his windowsill.

What had started as a small leak had now become a full-blown attack of dry rot and necessitated ripping all the plaster off the walls, removing window frames, skirting boards and floorboards, and replacing the carpet.

Demanding Tenants

At the other extreme, some tenants seem to think that you are always sitting at the end of the phone, day and night, just waiting for their call, and that it is your role in life to rush around to change light bulbs or unblock vacuum cleaners.

It reminds me of the way some young children go into catatonic shock when they see one of their teachers in the supermarket and realize for the first time that they are real people with real lives.

One female called me to say the broom was "no good". I presumed she meant it was broken, so I went to the property with the intention of repairing or replacing it. I looked at the broom and could find nothing wrong with it.

"But it doesn't sweep," she moaned. I thought I was missing something so I picked up the broom and started sweeping, then handed to her. She held it rather awkwardly and looked at me. "So, are you supposed to push it or pull it?" she asked.

The same tenant complained a few weeks later about the kitchen sink being blocked. The plumbing was all brand-new before she and her friends had moved in and, when I went to inspect, I found the waste pipes full of rice and other food scrapings.

I explained to her that this wasn't a waste-disposal unit and that waste food needed to be scraped into the bin, not into the sink.

Twice more that year the pipes had to be unblocked, so the tenants were charged for the work – a lot!

So, one of the first things I tell tenants is not to call me outside normal 'office' hours unless it's an emergency.

Some, including many parents, don't take any notice of this and think it's absolutely fine to disturb my evening with trivial enquiries.

Clearly, there is a balance to be struck here and, while I certainly discourage out-of-hours calls and warn that I will charge for unblocking vacuum cleaners and the like, nevertheless, I am anxious to keep my properties in good condition and be perceived as a responsive landlord.

If the job is for one for my contractors, I always phone them as soon as the problem is reported and get an estimate from them of when they will be able to attend. I then call the tenants and tell them when the job will be done, and suggest they call me back if it doesn't happen.

Emergencies

Of course, the most urgent job is when the boiler stops working and my marvellous gas man Raj usually attends within hours or at the very latest the next day.

If the boiler breaks down in very cold weather and cannot be repaired within 24 hours, it's a good idea to have half a dozen space heaters at the ready to take into the property so that the tenants can keep warm. These don't cost much and it's surprising how often you need them.

Even though the breakdown may be beyond your control, and your gas man is doing what he can, you do have a contractual responsibility to provide your tenants with a habitable property, and sub-zero temperatures are not habitable. Moreover, if you offer these heaters to your tenants before they actually ask for help, they will love you for it.

The other urgent breakdown is when a freezer gives up the ghost. Even though I warn tenants to insure their freezer contents, I do try to respond quickly when this happens because it can be very upsetting for the tenants, and so I always have a spare freezer in my garage (together with the space heaters!) for just such an eventuality.

Other, less urgent repairs are attended to as quickly as possible, and certainly within a few days. Not only do I want the properties to remain in good condition – I don't ever want to be in the position of having a tenant withholding rent on the grounds that a reported problem was not repaired.

Right of Entry

Prior to entering a tenanted property, you need to establish an understanding with your tenants about what is acceptable to them and to you regarding your right of entry.

They are the legal occupants and so they have the right to expect to be left to enjoy their occupancy without 'let or hindrance' from you. But clearly there are occasions when you need to enter either at their request or for your own purposes.

If it is at their request to attend to a breakdown, for example, I explain to my tenants that my contractors will come armed with a set of keys, and if there is no one in, they will let themselves in, do the repair, and then lock up on leaving. I have never had a problem with this, and tenants seem to accept it as reasonable.

If I wish to enter for my own purposes, for example, to show around prospective tenants for the following year, then I always give 24 hours' notice.

Strictly speaking, this should be in writing and to all tenants, but this is where having a good relationship comes in handy. If your tenants perceive you as being a helpful, responsive, friendly and cheerful person they will have no objection to a slight bending of the rules on this. So in reality, all I have to do when wishing to conduct a viewing is to send a text message to one of the tenants the day before, asking if they will please tell the others that I am coming, and that does the trick.

There have been many occasions when the others didn't actually get the message, and yet I was still granted entry.

On only one occasion did I get a complaint. I had two flats, one on top of the other. Early one Sunday morning I received a very distraught call from a female in the bottom flat saying that water was pouring through the ceiling on to her bed. I immediately called the guy in the top flat but got no response. So I rushed around and rang his bell – no answer, so I let myself in, went into the kitchen, and found the tap running and the kitchen sink over-flowing.

As I attended to it, a bleary-eyed tenant emerged from the bedroom and wanted to know "what the !#$*" I was doing in his kitchen at 8.30 on a Sunday morning.

I explained, saying that I had tried calling and tried ringing the doorbell. He continued to be abusive so, having attended to the problem, I then left.

I later wrote him a letter telling him I had right of entry without notice in an emergency and that this was most certainly an emergency. I then billed him for repairs to the downstairs ceiling and for my time in attending on a Sunday morning.

When the Tenants Are Away

There are two problems with having empty properties – they earn no money and there is no one present to look after them.

An empty property in the summer is less of a worry because, although it can be broken into and be occupied by squatters, at least it doesn't need heating.

Once the tenants have moved in, the property is their responsibility for the duration of the tenancy but, being young and inexperienced, they do need advice on what steps to take when they leave the property unoccupied.

You may get some tenants who ask for a discount or rebate for the Christmas break when they are going to be away, to which your response is a firm "No way, Jose"!

On the contrary, not only have they signed up for the duration but they actually remain responsible for the property whether or not they choose to live in it. The fact is, though, that most leave for two or three weeks at Christmas and that's the very time of the year when the property is at its most vulnerable.

The local villains tend to be most short of cash around Christmas time, and look out for properties where the family has gone to the winter sun or where students have gone home to mum's cooking.

So I tell my tenants not to leave anything in the property that might be attractive to thieves. If I am going to be around during the break, I offer to look after items brought to me for safe keeping, under the strict understanding, of course, that I am doing it as a personal favour and can't be held responsible.

I also give written advice on how to leave the property. The first, and most important piece of advice, is that they do not turn off the central heating, but re-set the timer so that it switches on for two bursts of about an hour a day so that, in very cold weather, pipes don't freeze. I warn that if there is a burst due to the property being allowed to get too cold, the tenants will be responsible for any subsequent damage and repairs.

To date, I've never had a burst pipe. I also advise that if a fridge-freezer is being turned off and defrosted, the door should be left open otherwise, on their return, the tenants will come back to a rich crop of mushrooms!

Deterring Burglars

I mentioned earlier that there is little that can be done to prevent a burglar who is determined to gain entry to a property but there are things that can be done to deter him.

Firstly, all curtains should be drawn so that someone from the outside cannot look into the rooms and thus spot things they would like to steal.

Secondly, it helps if a lamp is plugged into a pre-set timer so that it comes on during the evening and gives out the glow of habitation. Plugging in a radio to a timer also gives the sound of habitation.

Even though all my bedroom doors are fitted with locks, I advise against locking these while everyone is away, because there is nothing like a locked door to interest a burglar, and the damage caused by doors being smashed down is expensive and distressing. In the summer, I remind tenants to shut windows and draw curtains before they go off to their lectures.

Relationships with the University & Local Authority

If you choose to have your properties listed or accredited, you will have regular dialogue with the accommodation unit of the university (more often you chasing them than the other way around). If you have licensed properties, you will also meet 'officers', as they like to call themselves, from the local authority's housing department.

While it's obviously important to establish a good relationship with these people, bear in mind that they are all just cogs in a bureaucratic machine. Even middle managers are rarely capable of independent thought, but are programmed to repeat council policy endlessly, even when it is screamingly obvious that it is flawed.

I recently had a telephone conversation with a council tax officer who had sent me a demand for a student property. It went something like this:

Me: "Hello, you've sent me a demand instead of an application for renewing exemption. Why is that?"

Moronic Automaton: "Because the student courses ended in June, so it is Council policy to end the exemption."

Me: "Yes, I know the student courses ended in June, but you usually let the exemption carry though the summer and send out application forms for new exemption in October. Why haven't you done that with this property?"

Moronic Automaton: "Because the student courses ended in June, so it is Council policy to end the exemption."

Me: "Yes, you've already said that but my question is, why did you send a demand for this particular property and not all the others I own, where students also ended their courses last June?"

Moronic Automaton: "Because the student courses ended in June, so it is Council policy to end the exemption."

Me: "But you didn't end the exemption for the other properties, so what I'm trying to find out is why you ended it for this one."

Moronic Automaton: "Because the student courses ended in June, so it is Council policy to end the exemption."

Me: "Hello? Is there anyone there? Are you a real person? Do I need to select another option?"

Moronic Automaton: (sounding slightly flustered) "I can send you a new application form."

Me: "Oh, you've changed the tape haven't you! That was clever! I didn't even press a button! So, I'll bin this demand then and wait for the application form to arrive, shall I? But can you please just run this past your line manager and ask why I received this demand, or maybe you know the answer?"

Moronic Automaton: "Because the student courses ended in June, so it is Council policy to end the exemption."

Me: "I thought you might say that!"

This was the Council tax department, but I have it on very good authority that all local council officers are cloned in the same laboratory deep under the bowels of every civic centre in the land.

So if you want your properties approved, inspected, listed, or anything else, you need to play by their rules, understand what it is they need to know, so that they can tick all the boxes on their clipboards and, unlike me, try not to be too difficult.

Whether your property is being inspected against the criteria for an accreditation or licence, or by council tax officials, health and safety inspectors or environmental health officers – the varieties of local authority clones seems endless, even though they speak *withonevoice* – it's advisable to find out in advance what it is they're looking for and to prepare yourself thoroughly.

Handling Complaints

You may also be contacted if someone makes a complaint against you, and be prepared for the fact that the odds are heavily stacked against you from the start.

Many years ago one of my tenants didn't understand something in his tenancy agreement, but instead of coming to me for simple clarification, he popped into the local authority's housing department for advice.

They contacted me asking if I could go in with a copy of the tenancy agreement. They wouldn't tell me on the phone what the query was about, and asked me not to speak to the tenant in the meantime.

When I arrived at the council offices, I had to wait in a queuing system for over an hour and was then called to a counter.

The young woman looked coldly at me and asked for the tenancy agreement. I handed it over and watched her lip curl in disgust as she held it gingerly between two fingers at arm's length before dropping it into an in tray.

And that was that. I never did find out what the query was about, or why it was necessary to go in person. Feeling bemused, I turned back on leaving and asked whether her section acted as a conciliation service between landlords and tenants, to which her curt reply was "No, we just prosecute landlords". It was like the Voice of Doom.

I heard nothing more about the tenant's query but I was left in no doubt that, even though there are whole rafts of legislation in place to protect tenants, this council saw itself as very much on their side. It had institutionalised the notion that landlords are always the villains by creating a department whose sole function was to prosecute landlords. Nice to know how my council tax is spent!

Another organisation that may contact you on behalf of tenants is the Students' Union and, over the years, I have earned a grudging respect from my local Students' Union by standing up to them with numerous 'colourful' letters.

It is a pity that the Union seems to adopt an adversarial rather than a co-operative approach towards landlords.

There have been many occasions when I have actually referred tenants to them for help on a range of personal matters and gone out of my way to be flexible when tenants have been unable to pay rent. But on the few occasions when a tenant has gone to the Union with a complaint, the letter I get is anything but co-operative.

In every case the Union has made judgments about me based only on the student's account rather than checking with me first and getting both sides of the story.

In one instance, they even had the cheek to claim they had made an 'independent assessment' of a situation and judged me to be at fault. I pointed out that they had heard only one side of the story and, in any case, how could they claim to be independent when it was their role to represent students. Even their letterhead bore the slogan 'Putting Students First'.

Dealing with Aggressive Student Unions

I always meticulously keep copies of letters and emails sent to students and their guarantors, so in each case I was able to show that the student's account was, at best, economical with the truth, and the Union backed off.

But on other occasions, the Union has resorted to bullying and intimidation, citing non-existent laws to try to wear me down. That tactic might work with less-informed landlords who are wary of anyone in 'authority', but for me, it is like a red rag to a bull.

One 'law' often quoted was that of my 'duty of care', an emotive term, if ever there was one. I have already mentioned the case where the Union misguidedly advised a parent to defend my action against her for non-payment of rent on the basis that I had not shown her daughter proper 'duty of care' by sorting out a squabble between tenants.

On another occasion, a female who had left a tenancy prematurely had gone to the Union for advice, and they wrote to me

110

"reminding" me that I had a "duty of care to mitigate my own losses by finding a replacement tenant".

The logic of that completely escapes me.

Were they saying it's OK for a tenant to walk away from a freely-entered-into tenancy agreement? That it's the landlord's job to say, "There, there, that's OK, you go ahead and walk away from your contractual obligations and here, maybe you'd like a cuddle and some cash to take with you!"

I really cannot see how or why I am supposed to show 'duty of care' to someone in breach of contract, or what, exactly, that 'duty of care' should be.

The Students' Union also once wrote to me telling me I couldn't charge tenants for removing their bags of rubbish at the end of a tenancy unless I had registered the rubbish as 'trade waste'. They said I should also have obtained a certificate from the local council confirming that the rubbish had been disposed of properly and in accordance with some obscure European directive. What a load of rubbish!

This was mischief-making of the highest order by the Union, suggesting that domestic waste should be classed as trade waste, and thus put obstacles in the way of a landlord to prevent him charging tenants for its disposal. I ignored the letter, of course.

On another occasion, I had launched a case against a defaulting parent using the money claim website www.moneyclaim.gov.uk, which is the website for small claims in the county court.

When the parent went to the Union for advice, I received a wordy three-page letter from the 'Advice and Support Manager', whose letter also told me she was a Justice of the Peace, accusing me of being intimidating by launching a claim in the Northampton County Court, rather than in my local court.

Despite being a JP, she obviously didn't know that all online claims are handled by the Northampton Court and that, in any case, a defendant always has the option to transfer a case to their home court. It was this degree of ignorance, coupled with the arrogance, that epitomised all the correspondence I have received from the Students' Union.

On yet another occasion, a tenant wanted to get out of her tenancy agreement so that she could go and live with her boyfriend (I was told this by the other tenants).

But she got her father to write to the Students' Union telling them that she was so distressed with the untidiness of the other tenants and their constant marijuana smoking that she was giving up her course and going abroad. She said her landlord had failed to act on her numerous complaints, so she felt justified in leaving.

Instead of contacting me first to check her story, the Union accepted everything at face value and wrote to me "reminding" me that my "condoning of drug use" in my properties was strictly against "the rules of occupation", referring me to Section (d) of the Misuse of Drugs Act 1971.

This was the first I'd heard of any problems in that particular house, the tenants having been together for 18 months. I went to speak to the other tenants and found them outraged that they had been accused behind their backs of being untidy and of smoking marijuana. I certainly found no sign of it in the property and so I wrote to the Union suggesting, yet again, that they check their facts before rushing to judgment.

It turned out that the slur on me for "condoning" drug use emanated from one of my guidance documents in which I advised that "smoking" (meaning tobacco, of course) in my properties is permissible ,subject to all tenants agreeing where and when it can happen. But in the tenancy agreement, it is also made abundantly clear that the property should not be used for any illegal purposes.

Yet again, the Union retreated with a red face when presented with a full story. I was able, at a later date, to establish that the tenant concerned was living, not abroad, but with her boyfriend in the street next to the Union offices. I got every penny of rent owing from her.

So, you'll gather from all this that I have little respect for the expertise of my local Students' Union and deplore the way they bluff their way through legislation to try to get the upper hand, and bully landlords. And then they have the cheek to accuse a landlord of intimidation!

The irony is that recently, they actually referred some tenants to me for advice and help in mounting a court case against someone who had defrauded them, saying how experienced I was in such matters. I guess that's the nearest I'll ever get to an acknowledgement of their past mistakes.

Problem Parents

Sometimes, parents may also complain, although this is extremely rare.

All teachers will tell you (and I was one once) that they get little respect from complaining parents because everyone has been to school and so everyone believes themselves to be an expert on education.

A plumber, on the other hand, is regarded with awe and reverence as he open his toolbox full of magical implements, and practises his dark arts, re-igniting in seconds a boiler that stubbornly resisted for hours all the efforts of a mere mortal. But there's no mystique in being a landlord, is there? Anyone can do it, can't they? I mean, we've all lived in houses, most of us have bought one, so we're all experts, aren't we?

I had a letter from a parent last year complaining that I had charged his daughter from her deposit because she hadn't cleaned her room on leaving. He said he "knew for a fact" that her room was much cleaner on leaving than when she had moved in.

He suggested that I send her back the money I had deducted as a matter or urgency, and thus save us the trouble and expense of "going to our solicitors". He ended his letter menacingly, saying, "I am the senior estate manager in an international company, so I know how these things work".

It reminded me of the time, many years ago, when I was coaching my school football team and was confronted by a parent whose son I hadn't selected for the team. He looked at me squarely and said: "You know nothing about football, nothing! It would embarrass you if I told you how much I know about football!" He never did embarrass me.

So I wrote to Mr Senior Estate Manager who knew how it worked, reminding him, that how it works is this. On moving in, if he or his daughter had complaints about the cleanliness of her room, then they should have contacted me then, rather than leave it for nine months.

Surely he remembered, I said, that when she moved in, she and her friends were the first tenants in the house, it having been completely refurbished and re-decorated from scratch. She'd had a new bed and new carpet etc. so it was actually impossible for the room ever to have been cleaner than the day she moved in.

Needless to say, I never did hear from Mr Senior Estate Manager's solicitor.

He wasn't the only 'expert' to write to me. When a female student from whom I had taken a deposit failed to turn up at the beginning of the tenancy, resulting in my having to find a replacement, she lost the deposit in lieu of rent because the replacement wasn't found for three weeks.

Her father wrote to me telling me that he also had a buy-to-let property, and said: "I am an expert in these matters, and you are a little turd." The Little Turd chose not to reply to the Expert, and heard nothing more.

A mother called me a couple of years ago saying she was "most unhappy" with the house into which her son had just moved. I responded saying I was very sorry to hear that because I had been in the house only the day before and all the lads there seemed very happy.

Her: "They may be happy, but I'm not."

Me: "Oh, so what exactly is the problem?"

Her: "The sitting room and kitchen are far too small."

What could I say to that? Here's what I said, with what I wanted to say in brackets:

Me: "Oh, well, the problem is that some houses have big bedrooms but small communal rooms, like this one, and others have smaller bedrooms but big communal rooms."

(Me: "Oh, don't worry, I'll have them both extended by Friday")

Her: "But how can they all cook at the same time in that kitchen?"

Me: "Maybe they could organise a rota, or cook for one another, like other students often do."

(Me: "They don't all cook at the same time, you stupid woman!")

Her: "Well, I don't think it's good enough. And there's no dining table so they can't sit down properly for meals together."

Me: "Well, you know how it is, people very often eat meals on their laps watching TV, or take them to their rooms."

(Me: "No problem, I'll extend out into the street and build a new dining room too.")

Her: "That's not very hygienic. I think you should provide them with another house that is bigger."

Me: "Well, they did actually choose that house. I seem to remember that they looked at two or three back in February and liked that house because the bedrooms are so big."

(Me: "On your bike, Mrs Moaner.")

Her: "Well, I'm not satisfied. I will tell my son to withhold his rent until something is done."

Me: "Why don't I go to have a word with your son and the other tenants, and see if we can't sort this out?"

(Me: "You do that and I'll pull out all of his toenails very slowly, and then take you to court, demanding capital punishment.")

By the time I arrived at the house the mother had already spoken to the son, a lovely lad, who apologised profusely for his mother's intervention, saying that he and the others loved the house and had no problems about the kitchen or sitting room. Some parents can be a terrible embarrassment to their kids.

Tony's Tips

- Consider charging penalties to tenants persistently late with their rent.

- Record rent received in triplicate.

- Make sure that tenants leaving prematurely know that they must continue paying rent until a replacement is found.

- Tell tenants not to call you outside office hours except in an emergency.

- Make sure repairs are done as quickly as possible and monitor the work of your contractors.

- Keep a spare fridge-freezer and space heaters for emergencies.

- Make sure tenants understand that they are responsible for damage if they allow the property to freeze up during winter.

- Co-operate with all the various agencies, like the Students' Union, but stand up for yourself when they complain – they are often wrong.

Chapter 9

Ending the Tenancies

If you are concerned that your tenants may not vacate at the end of the tenancy you should issue them with a formal notice to quit (Section 21 notice). To make it stick in court, a similar notice should have preceded it at the beginning of the tenancy.

In my experience, students do not overstay their welcome in any sort of malicious way, although you may get one or two asking if they can extend by a couple of weeks to finish some research or take extra exams.

Provided this doesn't encroach on the next tenancy or mess up cleaning schedules, and that they pay the extra rent up front, this is not a problem, of course. The only time I have resorted to using the Section 21 notice is when I have been selling a property, and so wanted to be absolutely sure that the tenants would be gone on time. And they were, of course.

At around the same time – two months before the end of the tenancy – I send a letter reminding the tenants of the end date and giving detailed advice on how the property should be handed back to me if they wish to avoid charges against their deposit.

This is the one time in the year when tenants really respond promptly and positively to something I send out. The mention of 'charges against deposits' seems to focus the mind wonderfully, and I am always pleasantly surprised at the efforts gone to by even the most untidy of tenants to make sure that I have no justification for making a charge.

Problems sometimes arise when some tenants leave earlier than others, and those remaining are left to clear up the communal areas. Some do but many others don't, feeling rather put upon to be left to do all the heavy cleaning.

I make it quite clear that I will charge individuals for their own room, and split the cost of any charges against communal areas between all tenants equally, regardless of who left early. I explain that I have no other way of doing it and that if they have a complaint about the fairness of such a system, then they should sort it out between themselves.

So what I request is that all furniture should be returned to original locations, posters and Blu-tac removed from walls and holes in walls filled and painted. All surfaces must be dusted and wiped, the fridge-freezer defrosted and cooker cleaned, floors vacuumed and mopped, rubbish removed from the premises, and missing items replaced.

It's a long list and wishful thinking to expect it all to be done, but it provides a useful check list and most tenants do make an honest attempt to address it.

The item they consistently fail on is to remove all rubbish, simply because the bin men won't take away all the stuff they have accumulated over a year or two, and they rarely have their own transport to take it to the local dump.

I warn that dirty cookers will incur a heavy charge, and that any rental items must be removed before they go. I also ask for all keys to be left in bedrooms, together with a stamped addressed envelope for the return of deposits. The last person leaving is also expected to read the meters but I always do this again anyway during my inspection.

The Final Inspection

Given that the tenants all leave at different times, and that I may not be available at exactly the time the last one is leaving, it is very rarely that I do an inspection with a tenant present. The tenant has the right to insist on that, of course, but only if a mutually convenient time can be arranged.

So far, no one has ever insisted on accompanying me, and now that digital photography is with us, I take snaps of properties that are particularly untidy, just in case there should be a challenge, but it rarely happens.

When entering the property, armed with a copy of the inventory, I start at the top, working my way down. It is important to write the name of each room's former occupant on the inventory so that when you come to make charges against each person, you can be sure to have the right room and right person.

If you can't remember which person occupied which room, the stamped addressed envelope left behind will help you. In each bedroom, I turn the bed on its side to check that cleaning has been thorough – under the majority of beds I find a massive hoard of unmentionables, the bagging up and disposing of which, is a chargeable item, of course.

Having ticked off the contents of a room against the inventory and checked that a full set of keys has been left (and that they are the right keys and not just any old bunch left behind in lieu!), I check for damage.

Some tenants go to great lengths to conceal damage, so it is necessary to move furniture around and to be thorough in the examination. I make a note of the amount of rubbish, the lack of cleaning, the damage, the missing keys, the soiled mattress etc, and move on to the next room.

In the sitting room I check under the cushions of the chairs and settees to see that the springs are still intact. In the kitchen I check the cleanliness of the cooker, whether the fridge-freezer has been defrosted, and whether the contents of the cupboards are present and reasonably clean.

Quite often a lot of food is left behind, but this must be disposed of, so it is chargeable. Next I check the condition of the bathroom and lastly, the cellar and outside areas, where I am most likely to find an accumulation of bags of rubbish or other discarded items.

Even in a house where there is quite a lot of rubbish and some damage, I don't necessarily impose charges. It's really a question of using judgment. If they have, in every other respect, been good tenants, paid their rent on time, been friendly and polite, and have made a reasonable attempt to clean up, then I always feel it would be churlish of me to bang on heavy charges for cleaning and repairs.

If, on the other hand, the tenants have been nothing but trouble from beginning to end, then I view this as my last chance to get my own back and feel justified in sticking rigidly to the provisions in the contract that allow me to impose charges.

But whether or not I am being lenient or tough, I always send every tenant a full account of what charges are being made and put this in the stamped addressed enveloped, together with their cheque, or without the cheque if the charges exceed the deposit held.

The final account shows the amount of deposit held and then lists the charges applied to the communal areas, divided equally between all tenants. Next, it lists charges applied to the tenant's own room, and finally charges relating to non-payment or late payment of rent, or to other items not already covered.

I then total this up, deduct it from the deposit held, and send a cheque for the balance. In actual fact, most of my tenants get their deposit back in full but, at the other extreme, some get nothing back at all, and where they show a negative balance, I ask them to send me a cheque to settle the account.

Where the amount owing is less than £100, I then forget about it, and few send it. But if the amount is much greater than that, then I embark on recovery procedures, involving letters to the tenant and the guarantor, and eventually may have to consider making a claim in the county court. Thankfully, this happens very rarely and certainly not every year.

Preparing For the Next Set of Tenants

At the same time as checking the inventory, I bag up the rubbish and remove it from the property. Where there are large amounts, I take a photo, just in case there should be any denial, and use my trailer to take it all to the dump.

The house is then ready for cleaning, and in goes my cleaner, Svetlana. A day later I go back in with a paintbrush and box of tools to attend to minor repairs, re-do the inventory, put up the new notices, replace missing keys and worn-out furniture, and then the property is ready again for occupation.

Where tenants stay on for a second year (and most of my tenants do that) then I do nothing in the summer between their two years because, even though they may have gone away, their belongings are still in the property.

They have paid rent or retainers, so the property remains their responsibility. I remind them to shut windows, draw curtains and to lock up. The only thing left for me to do is to call at the property every couple of weeks to clear mail away from the front door so that potential burglars aren't alerted to the fact that the property is empty.

Tony's Tips

- Send a letter to tenants giving detailed advice on how you want the property handed back.

- When inspecting at the end of the tenancy, take digital photos.

- Send out a full final account, itemising any charges.

- If the mess left behind is only minor and the tenants were good, waive the charges.

Chapter 10

Record Keeping

I've already mentioned the importance of keeping good records of the rent you receive so that, if challenged, you are able to provide clear and unambiguous evidence that you did or did not receive payments.

But vigilant record-keeping is essential in everything you do because you will be surprised how often you need to refer back to a particular incident or to find a document. It is essential that you have a good filing system, keeping hard copies of everything in case your computer records are wiped out. Perhaps the two most crucial areas of record-keeping are health and safety, and accounts.

Health and Safety

When you have your properties inspected for gas and electrical safety you will be given copies of certificates, one to be displayed in the property, and another for your own records.

You will need to make sure that none of your certificates expires while the properties are still tenanted, so keep records of expiry dates, and organise new inspections in good time. Bear in mind that if you leave it to the last minute, your gas engineer or electrician might be away on holiday when you need them.

If applying for accreditation or licensing, you will be asked to send in your certificates for examination, so make copies, and file them away carefully and methodically so that they can easily be retrieved at a later date.

Keep records of all reports of damage or breakdown in a property and notes of how each one was dealt with so that if a tenant or parent wishes to complain that you have not attended properly to repairs, you can quote authoritatively from your records.

On rare occasions, where there were early signs of difficult tenants in properties, I have kept logs recording every visit and every communication to a property, just in case, at some later date,

I might be required to provide evidence of what had actually happened.

In the case of the parents who accused me of not sorting out tenants' squabbles in a house, the log became court evidence and the judge said how impressed he was by what I had done to help the tenants.

Also keep copies of all letters from the local council, the university and other organisations. There is nothing more frustrating than trying to respond to an 'official' enquiry only to discover that you cannot lay your hand on a vital letter you sent months before.

You would thus be unable to prove that you had complied with an earlier request or be able to put your side of a story.

Accounts

If you do not have one already get yourself a good accountant. They say a good accountant earns her fee by the amount she saves you in tax.

In my case, my accountant, Ermintrude, saves me nothing, but stops me getting into trouble by holding me back from claiming expenses that are not allowable, or which might give rise to unwanted attention from the tax inspector.

In the early days of my property business, my previous accountant, Errol, explained to me that tax collection is an art, not a science, and that the rules were open to all sorts of interpretation, hence the massive industry in tax avoidance.

He said it was essential that I kept receipts for all the work done by my contractors, and good records of all other forms of expenditure.

But when it came to petty cash items, provided what I was claiming sounded reasonable, it was not necessary to keep receipts for every tiny pot of paint. WRONG, Errol!

While some tax inspectors might be reasonable, and take an artistic, rather than scientific approach to such matters, he wasn't reckoning on Miss D Meanour, the tax inspector (former KGB agent?) who chose me for a tax enquiry a few years later.

These enquiries are done at random and anyone can get one at any time, so I am told. How it happens is a big finger suddenly appears in the sky pointing at your house, and a booming voice says "It could be you!" It was me.

Miss D Meanour demanded paper evidence of every single item of expenditure for a previous tax year. While I had no problem with all the larger items, I was sent scrabbling into bank and credit card accounts, cheque books, biscuit tins, and everywhere I could think of to find proof of what I had spent.

The irony is that I believed, and still believe, the amounts claimed were based on what I had actually spent. But after weeks of searching, there remained about £1,200 of spending for which I simply could not provide receipts, and even though this was for items bought at car boot sales, from junk shops, off the back of vans etc, the tax inspector was having none of it.

So you'll be thinking, well, £1,200 isn't much to pay out of a big rental turnover, so what's the problem? Pay the money, and that's that, isn't it?

No, it isn't, because then what Miss D Meanour did, as they are prone to do, was assume that I had been over-claiming by a similar amount for the previous seven years so, with interest added, the figure owed suddenly jumped to £10,000.

But the cloud had a silver lining. Errol warned me that, on top of the £10,000, she could slap on extra penalties for evasion, which could easily double the figure.

But it was at that point Errol really earned his money. He was able to persuade Miss D Meanour that I had fully co-operated with the enquiry and there was no evidence to suggest that I had deliberately under-paid my tax.

He said the amount concerned in any one year was very small indeed, so she decided to settle for the £10,000 and not ask for penalties.

124

I was lucky and since that date I have kept every single tiny receipt. When I submit my accounts, I make sure they are so thorough and complete that they can withstand challenge from even the most tenacious tax inspector.

Taxcafe.co.uk has produced many excellent books on managing your tax affairs, so I will not go into detail here on this subject.

Suffice it to say there are a number of expenses you can legitimately claim against your income when submitting your accounts, and this will reduce significantly the amount of tax you have to pay.

Here is a list of the expenses I claim:

- Accountancy fees
- Travelling expenses
- Postage and stationery
- Telephone
- Cleaning
- Insurance
- Gardening
- Professional association fees
- Light and heat
- Loan interest
- Wear and tear allowance (which is 10% of your gross takings on a property)
- Advertising and promotion
- Agents' charges (if you use one)
- Council tax (if you have to pay any which you cannot re-charge to tenants)
- Water rates (unless the tenants pay this)
- Sundry other expenses (cleaning, decorating materials etc) and repairs and renewals (which include all contractors' bills).

You can also claim for use of a room in your house as an office. That will include the lighting and heating of that room and for capital expenditure on items such as computers.

Other items you can claim tax relief on will include your van and trailer and even things like your mobile phone! Your accountant will advise you on the details.

Selling

Eventually, the time comes for you to hang up your J-cloth and retire to Dunlettin', and so you will want to start selling up your portfolio.

I love buying properties but I hate selling them. Buying has all the excitement of getting a good deal, growth, expansion, restoration and the prospect of earning more money.

Selling is always the point of realisation when you find the property is not worth as much as you thought and when surveyors and viewers point out blemishes. This is when people mess you around and waste your time by failing to turn up for viewings, or back out of a deal after months of prevarication, when lenders go on holiday just when everyone is waiting for a mortgage offer to come through, and so on. Anyone who has sold a house knows the picture.

When selling a house that is set up for student tenants, you need to decide which market you are going for. Do you wait until the tenants have gone and then sell it as a family home 'with vacant possession' or do you sell it fully tenanted to another landlord?

In my experience, the latter is a much safer bet because landlords like the idea of buying a house that will earn money from day one. But don't expect to get a price above market value because it is tenanted and furnished. On the contrary, landlords will try to bid you down by 20-30% for 'taking it off your hands'!

Watch out for Tax Scams

When I was selling some properties last year I was offered a tax scam on at least three occasions. It works likes this. You reach an agreed sale price of, say, £150,000, and you have a capital gains tax liability of £20,000.

The buyer offers to buy the property for £100,000 'on the record' thus reducing your capital gains tax liability. He then says he will give you a further £40,000 in cash in a brown envelope, the idea being that you will save £10,000 in CGT and he will get the property for £10,000 cheaper.

DON'T FALL FOR THIS! This is tax evasion (illegal) and not tax avoidance. And it is you, not the buyer, who is taking all the risks.

Capital Gains Tax Planning

But you can save yourself capital gains tax legally when selling up if, when you bought the properties in the first place, you have registered some properties in the names of other members of your family.

Anyone over the age of 18 can own a property in the UK and everyone is entitled to an annual tax allowance, set against income, a basic-rate tax band and an annual allowance against the disposal of a capital asset.

So if you have property in the name of a child who is perhaps at university and not yet employed, you can not only save money on the tax payable on the rent received from a property in your child's name but also on CGT due when you come to sell the property.

If you spread the sale of a portfolio over two or three tax years, you can save a lot in CGT because each owner is entitled to the CGT allowance every year.

Beware, when selling up, the vultures calling themselves 'financial advisers', who charge mega-bucks for telling you about 'secret' offshore tax havens where you can move to avoid CGT altogether.

One tried to persuade me to part with £40,000 for his advice (which he called 'intellectual property'!). I suggested a deal. I would tell him the name of the best street in which to buy a student house in exchange for him telling me the name of the desert island where I should take my money.

I reasoned that if his intellect was worth £40,000, mine was worth at least that much, but he wasn't amused. It turned out that my advice would have been more valuable, because a week later, the Chancellor announced a clampdown on the very scheme he was trying to sell me. You don't get a refund on intellectual property.

Tony's Tips

- Keep meticulous copies and records of everything.

- Keep all receipts, and claim all relevant expenditure against tax liability, including the price of this book!

- Avoid illegal or expensive schemes for reducing CGT liability.

Chapter 11

Final Words of Advice

When I used to write school inspection reports, it was always customary to say a few nice things at the end, but then follow the nice things with recommendations for the school, the local authority, and others involved in the running of the school, so as to bring about improvements.

Those recommendations were later used as the basis for action plans. I see no reason why I shouldn't end this book in the same way.

A Few Nice Things

The overwhelming majority of students are great tenants, and returns from student properties are high. Students pay their rent in full, if not always on time, and they look after properties very well.

The student housing market is here to stay and is growing, so there will always be scope for enterprising landlords who aspire to high standards and wish to develop a letting business, even in areas that may appear to be saturated with rental properties.

But landlords should not underestimate the amount of 'hands-on' work needed in the early stages of constructing a successful portfolio.

The most remarkable finding in this book is that overseas students account for between 14% and 30% of our university population, providing both the universities and landlords with a lucrative source of income, as well as enriching the cultural, intellectual and skill resources of our country.

Landlords, and the variety of contractors who assist them, are regenerating the country's housing stock and stimulating the economy.

Universities would not survive without their contribution, and the Government's policy to expand higher education would be a shambles.

Recommendations

For the sake of brevity, I am restricting myself to one recommendation for each target group.

Landlords should:
Always aspire to providing quality properties, good service, an impeccable code of conduct, and be fully responsive to the never-ending stream of housing legislation.

Universities should:
Recognise the unique contribution made by private landlords and, in the case of overseas students, enter into contractual rent guarantee arrangements.

Mortgage Lenders should:
Recognise the financial constraints under which students operate by allowing individual tenancy agreements in shared houses.

Surveyors should:
Reform and standardise their practice, making it more consistent, and providing valuations that enable, rather than disable, the conveyancing process.

The Government should:
Reform the small claims procedure, making it easier for claimants with judgments in their favour to get their money.

Student Unions, Accommodation Units, and Local Authorities should:
Seek to provide a genuine conciliation service between landlords and tenants instead of always assuming the tenant to be in the right.

And finally, a text message from a tenant, promising a rent payment which I wasn't over-enthusiastic about receiving...

Hi tony got ur txt. Cnt bring the £20 2day cos seths dog et it. lol. Shud get it bk 2mrw. Thx liam

Appendix A

Sample Letters & Documents

a) Letter to go out with new tenancy agreements

> 101 Rachman Ave.
> Cooltown,
> CL12 7GG

Dear Wanda & Co,

RE: 1, Campus View, Cooltown, CL1 6PR

I enclose two tenancy agreements (one to keep and one to return to me) and a rent guarantee form each. Could you please phone me when everything is ready and I will come to collect:

- One completed and signed tenancy agreement each
- One completed and signed rent guarantee each, and
- £160 deposit each (Please note that the £120 retainers are due in by May 1st)

If you want to move in for the summer, please ask me for a summer tenancy agreement. Your retainer will be offset against the summer rent.

Could you please ensure that I get everything back by 13th April. I will then give you letters confirming your tenancy.

Don't hesitate to ask any further questions and please refer your rent guarantors to my website: www.topdigs4u.co.uk. I am happy for parents to ring with their own questions.

With best wishes,

Ivor Castle

Wanda Palace,
Room 36,
Pokey Hall,
Cooltown University.

----

b) The Tenancy Agreement

ASSURED SHORTHOLD TENANCY AGREEMENT (ASH)

between   *Ivor Castle*   (the landlord)

and   *Wanda Palace*   (the tenant)

PLEASE READ THIS DOCUMENT CAREFULLY BEFORE SIGNING, AND TAKE ADVICE IF YOU HAVE ANY DOUBTS. SHOULD YOU NEED CLARIFICATION, PLEASE RING THE LANDLORD ON...........

Address of property being rented:

1, Campus View,
Cooltown,
CL1 6PR

(Details of our properties appear in *www.topdigs4u.co.uk*)

Scope of the tenancy
This tenancy is for exclusive use of one study bedroom, and shared use with other tenants, of communal areas including kitchens, bathrooms, sitting rooms, corridors and gardens.

Landlord's address and telephone:
101 Rachman Ave.
Cooltown,
CL12 7GG

Tel: 07967 555555
email: ivorcastle@topdigs4u.co.uk

Your home address and telephone:
Goodhome,
Guarantee Lane,
Much Smiling,
Thx

Tel: 01643 555555

Your mobile phone number: *07850 555555*

Your e-mail address: *tidywanda@yahoo.co.uk*

Your university course and year: *BA in Quiet Studies (year 2)*

Period of tenancy:
June 20th-Sep 11th – retention period (available for summer let)
Sep 12th 2006 to June 18th 2007 (40 assured short-hold tenancy)

Returnable Deposit:
You need to pay a returnable deposit of £160 when you sign this tenancy agreement. Your deposit will be lodged with the Government's Custodial Scheme and will be returned to you on completion of the tenancy, after you have discharged all your obligations as described in this agreement and vacated the property. The deposit is returned subject to *possible* deductions for:

1. Unpaid rent, interest for rent paid late, other unpaid bills or charges,
2. Items missing as listed on the inventory, or keys not returned
3. Cleaning and repairs to the property, if found to be necessary following an inspection after the property is vacated.

Please note that under the terms of this agreement, you cannot use your deposit to pay rent.

Retainer:
The property is available for you to rent for the summer (please ask for a summer contract if you would like to move in/remain during the summer). If you want the room reserved for you, a retainer of £10 per week is payable in lieu of summer rent.

Rent: (cheques payable to *I. Castle*)
Rent for the ASH tenancy period is **£2,800** (equivalent to **£70** per week) and is payable in the following instalments:

1. £1,120 on Tuesday 12th September 2006
2. £1,120 on Tuesday 2nd January 2007
3. £560 on Tuesday 24th April 2007

Rent should be posted to the landlord's address to arrive by the due date. **THIS IS MOST IMPORTANT**. If you are still awaiting funds on rent day you may send a cheque that is post-dated by up to two weeks *without prior arrangement*, but you are responsible for informing the landlord should your funds not be in place by the date written on the cheque. For delays that are expected to *exceed two weeks*, you *must* contact the landlord *before the rent is due* in order to discuss a possible re-scheduling of payment. A charge of £5 will be made for cheques that 'bounce'. Except when arranged in advance, rent or bills overdue by more than three days will be liable to a daily charge of £1 payable from the day when the rent was due.

If you prefer to pay rent in monthly instalments you may do so, but only if you are able to pay by standing order. If you wish to do this, please ask for a Standing Order Mandate. Regrettably, monthly payments by cheque are not acceptable. The rent will not be increased during the period of the tenancy.

The rent includes water rates, normal servicing, and gardening, but not the consumption of electricity, gas or telephone (see below).

Rent Guarantors:
If you are not in full-time employment you need to supply a signed undertaking from a person of appropriate financial status (usually a parent) who will act as guarantor for payment of rent and any other charges for the duration of the tenancy. A form for this purpose has been given to you with this tenancy agreement. Please have it completed, signed and returned as soon as possible.

Council Tax:
Full exemption from Council Tax is only granted when **all** of the tenants are full-time students. If one is a part-time student, then 75% of the council tax is payable. If two or more are part-time, then 100% is payable. These sums are payable by the tenants who are not full time students.

In order to apply for Council Tax exemption, the landlord will ask you to provide him with a photocopy of your enrolment form or a 'Council tax' letter provided by the University. These documents state whether your course is full or part-time. This will be needed as soon as possible after the start of the autumn term, and it **must** be provided in order to qualify for exemption.

Please note that you are signing a declaration at the end of this tenancy agreement saying you are a full-time student. Please amend this declaration if you are only part-time, or you may be in breach of contract. If your student status changes after signing the agreement, please discuss this with the landlord as soon as possible

Inventory:
An inventory of contents in the property will be posted on the notice board at the commencement of the tenancy. You should check this list at the time of moving in and contact the landlord immediately if there are any discrepancies.

Repairs:
Please keep the property in a clean condition and attend to accidental damage quickly. The walls in the house must not be re-decorated, and furniture should not be altered or removed. Light bulbs in hallways and corridors must be replaced promptly when they fail so as to keep the areas well-lit and safe. Tenants are collectively responsible for replacing consumable items (e.g. light bulbs and broken windows) and for unblocking waste pipes and drains.

The landlord will be responsible for all repairs other than those caused by negligence, misuse or avoidable accidents. Please keep the landlord informed should any repairs become necessary by telephoning 07967 555555. **Please try not to call outside normal working hours except in an emergency.** Should there be an emergency and it proves impossible to contact the landlord, the following approved contractors should be called out:

Gas appliances:	Raj the Plumber 07944 555555
Electrical installations:	Sparky the Electrician 07930 555555
All other repairs	Tom the Builder 07933 555555

Except in emergencies, tenants will bear collective responsibility for contractors' bills that have been incurred without the landlord's consent.

Landlord's access to the property:
Whenever you report a breakdown, either the landlord or his contractor will come as soon as possible and, if the property is vacant, they will use their keys to enter the property to undertake the repair.

If the landlord needs to come to the property for his own reasons (e.g. to show prospective tenants) he will always endeavour to give at least 24 hours' notice. Please note that the landlord has the right of immediate entry in the event of an emergency.

Gas, electricity and telephone:
You are responsible, with the other tenants, for making your own arrangements for gas, electricity and telephone. You must take readings when you first move in and register yourself with the utility suppliers. When you leave the property you must make arrangements for final bills to be sent to a forwarding address.

Pets, bicycles and ball games:
Please do not keep pets at the property. Bicycles should not be kept inside the house. You are strongly advised not to play ball games in the garden because these often result in damage to fencing or windows.

Insurance:
You are advised to insure your personal effects, including food and freezer contents, against damage, theft or breakdown. This can usually be appended to the insurance of your parents' home, where applicable.

Premature termination of contract:
Please note that this is a fixed-term tenancy and can only be terminated inside the contract period should either you or the landlord break the terms of the contract, in which case two months' notice will apply from the other side.

Should you request release from the contract for any other reason, this will be granted ***provided another tenant can be found to take up the unexpired portion of your tenancy***. This is your responsibility, although the landlord will help.

In these circumstances, you will remain responsible for meeting rent deadlines until the replacement tenant is found. The landlord may also make a small administration charge for arrangements connected with the replacement tenant.

Any overpaid rent or deposit held will be returned to you as soon as the new tenant has taken up the tenancy.

Declaration:

I, the tenant agree:

1. to maintain a courteous and considerate approach to the landlord
2. to pay the rent and other bills by the due date
3. to keep the property in good repair and in a clean condition, including communal areas
4. not to remove fixtures or fittings
5. to have due regard for the health and safety of others, particularly in respect of hygiene, fire prevention and use of electrical apparatus
6. to ensure that the property is secure when unoccupied
7. to take appropriate precautions against burst pipes when the property is left empty
8. to unstop the sinks, toilets and drains when blocked
9. to report any defects, damage or breakages promptly so that the landlord can take appropriate action to organise repairs
10. not to keep animals on the property, or bicycles in the house
11. to have consideration for other tenants and neighbours, especially with regard to noise levels and parking
12. to ensure that refuse is not kept on the property beyond the normal period of collection
13. with the exception of *occasional* overnight guests staying in my own room, not to sublet or part with possession of the property or any parts thereof without the consent of the landlord
14. to allow the landlord (or his contractors) reasonable access to the property in order that he can discharge his legal and contractual responsibilities
15. not to use the property for any illegal purposes
16. at the end of the tenancy, to leave the property in the same condition as when the tenancy commenced, fair wear & tear accepted

I agree to abide by the terms and conditions of this tenancy agreement, and I confirm that I will be engaged in a full-time course of study during the academic year 2006/2007

Signed: .... (tenant) Date: ....

138

I, the landlord agree:

1. to maintain a courteous and considerate approach to you and other tenants
2. to hand over the property and its contents at the commencement of the tenancy in a fit and proper condition
3. to respond promptly and efficiently to reports of defects or breakages, and to carry out repairs within a reasonable time span
4. to arrange annual safety checks of gas appliances and to display safety certificates
5. to apply, on your behalf, for any exemptions from Council Tax that are in force
6. to respond sympathetically, when requested, to any personal difficulties facing you, and to liaise with the Students' Union or other agencies, as appropriate.
7. to provide a full and detailed final account, showing any charges against your deposit, and to return the balance to you within ten days of the end of the tenancy.

I agree to abide by the conditions of this tenancy agreement and I confirm that I am the landlord of the property.

Signed:...(landlord) Date:..............

----

c) The Rent Guarantee

RENT GUARANTEE

Tenant's name... (please print)

Address of property being rented: ....
....
....

Tenant's home address: ....
....
....

Guarantor's declaration
I, the undersigned, hereby covenant with landlord of the above property, to guarantee payment of rent, council tax (if applicable) or any other legitimate charges as described in any tenancy agreements signed by the tenant.

Name .... (please print)

Signed .... Date:........................

Relationship to tenant ....

Address (if different to the tenant) ....
....
....

Telephone ....

Email ....

NB. The guarantor should be a person of suitable financial status who is able to honour the guarantee if called upon to do so. Tenants are warned that it is a criminal offence to use the name of a guarantor without their consent, or to forge their signature.

----

d) The Standing Order Mandate

<u>STANDING ORDER MANDATE</u>

TO: .... (Your bank's name and address)

     ....

     ....

     .... (Your bank's sort code)

RE: .... (Your account number)

Please pay **£311.11** on 12th September 2006, and thereafter on the 12th day of each month, with the final payment being due on 12th May 2007, to the following account:

ACCOUNT NAME: I. CASTLE
BANK: HSBC, PO BOX 66, COOLTOWN, CL12 7GG
CODE: 40 47 17
A/C NUMBER: 39921071

This standing order replaces any previous order for payments into this account.

SIGNED...............................   DATE....................

(Please send this form directly to your bank.)

---

e) Letter confirming tenancy

----

101 Rachman Ave.
Cooltown,
CL12 7GG

Dear *Wanda,*

RE: 1, Campus View, Cooltown, CL1 6PR

This is to confirm that I have reserved a room in the house for you subject to having received the following:

- your signed tenancy agreement
- your rent guarantee form
- your returnable deposit

Please do not delay in sending me any items above still outstanding; any delay could result in the house being offered to other tenants. Please telephone me should you have any queries.

Please note that your retainer is payable by May 1st, and should you opt to move in at the end of June, it will be offset against your summer rent. If you intend moving in at this time, please ask for a summer tenancy agreement.

Before you move in to the house, each room will be fully furnished but you will need to bring your own bedding.

The kitchen will be fully equipped with crockery, cutlery and cooking utensils but you may wish to bring your own microwave oven.

There is plumbing for an automatic washing machine, should you choose to hire or buy one (the out-going tenants may wish to sell theirs to you, or simply leave theirs behind, so wait until you move in before doing anything).

An inventory of house contents will be on the notice board, and you should check this carefully as, at the end of the tenancy, charges *may* be made for items missing.

Please also let me know when you are moving in so that I can arrange to meet you with keys.

I hope you will be happy in the house.

With best wishes,

Yours sincerely,

Ivor Castle.

----

f) Letter to guarantors, chasing late rent

----

101 Rachman Ave.,
Cooltown,
CL12 7GG

19th November 2006

Dear Mr and Mrs Palace,

Re: Wanda Palace, tenant at 1 Campus View – overdue rent.

I wrote to you recently regarding Wanda's rent, which should have been paid on September 12th, but you have not replied.

Despite numerous letters and messages, Wanda has still not paid the rent and is not responding to my messages. In my last letter, I asked if you would kindly speak to Wanda, but I have still heard nothing.

I have now reached the stage where I must ask you, as her rent guarantors, to pay the rent on her behalf, and I should be grateful if you would do so within the next seven days.

Should I not receive the payment by then, I will be left with no alternative other than to start proceedings in the County Court. This will not only add further fees to the amount already owed but may also result in your having a county court judgment against you.

This can adversely affect your credit rating and your ability to get loans or other finance. I am sure that you will wish to avoid this course of action, so I look forward to receiving payment from you in the next few days.

Thank you for your co-operation.

Yours sincerely,

Ivor Castle.

----

g) Letter inviting tenancy renewal for a 2nd year

----

101 Rachman Ave.
Cooltown,
CL12 7GG

12th December 2005

Dear Tenants,

Renewal of your tenancy for 2006-7

I am writing to ask whether you wish to renew your tenancy with me for the next academic year and stay on in one of my properties. It is my usual practice to give existing tenants the first option and, as I have already started to get enquiries from prospective tenants for next September, I need to know fairly soon if you want to stay on with me.

Your returnable deposit will be carried forward, so there will be no need to come up with any extra cash now, although there will be a summer retainer to pay for those of you not remaining in the property during the summer.

Those who wish to stay for the summer will be required to sign a summer tenancy agreement. You can leave all your belongings in the property over the summer if you wish and the utilities (gas and electricity) must be kept in your names for the summer period.

If you want to stay on where you are, simply email me or complete the slip below, and return it to me. One slip for all of you will suffice.

I will then send you new tenancy agreements for next year. If you would prefer to switch to another of my properties, give me a ring on 07967 401287 to discuss the options. Please let me have your decision by **20th January**. After that date I will offer your house to others.

Should you decide not to stay on, may I ask for your understanding and patience when I bring prospective tenants to view. I will always endeavour to arrange viewings at your convenience and try to give at least 24 hours' notice where possible.

I hope you are able to stay on next year and I look forward to hearing from you very soon.

Ivor Castle.

....

REPLY SLIP
(Send to Ivor Castle, 101 Rachman Ave. Cooltown, CL12 7GG)

NAME(S): ....
....
....

PROPERTY: ....
....
....

I/WE WOULD LIKE TO STAY ON IN 2006-2007.

----

h) Letter confirming arrangements for completing a tenancy

----

101 Rachman Ave.
Cooltown,
CL12 7GG

Dear *Wanda,*

I am writing to confirm arrangements for the completion of your tenancy.

As you know your contract expires on 18th June and you **must** leave the property by that date. If you intend to leave before then, please ring me to let me know the date on which the **last** person is leaving. This will speed up the return of your deposit.

Would you please leave a stamped addressed envelope **in your room** (unsealed, with your keys inside) when you go so that your deposit can be sent on to you. However, if you are moving to another of my properties, just leave a note with your keys so that I know whose room it is. This is most important.

The last person out should turn off all electrical appliances, including the central heating, make sure that all windows and doors are shut, lock up and put *their* keys back through the letter box.

Would the last person out please telephone me to say that the house is empty.

Please make sure the house is handed back in the **same condition** as when you moved in. The following check-list might prove helpful:

- Furniture returned to original locations
- Posters and Blue-tac removed from walls
- Holes in walls filled and painted
- Furniture and surfaces dusted and wiped
- Freezer/fridge defrosted and cleaned out
- Cooker cleaned thoroughly (the deduction for a dirty cooker is very large!)

- Floors vacuumed or mopped
- All rubbish removed from premises
- Missing/broken items replaced
- Rental items (e.g. washing machines) removed from premises
- Meters read on last day of occupation and gas/electricity companies given forwarding addresses for final bills. Please *do not* re-register the gas and electricity in my name – the new tenants will register when they move in. Please leave details of the suppliers on the notice board.

Please note deductions **may** be made from your deposit as follows:

- For rent unpaid, and additional expenses incurred in my having to collect rent
- For interest charged on those occasions when rent was late without prior agreement
- For items in the house that are missing or broken
- For repairs necessitated by misuse or carelessness, or unnecessary call-outs during the year
- For cleaning or damage, should the house not be left in a satisfactory condition
- For removal of rubbish, including unwanted belongings
- For expenses incurred liaising with utilities, rental co's etc.

If you are moving to another one of my properties next year, any deductions will be carried forward with your deposit for settlement at the end of next year.

If you are not returning, a final account and the remainder of your deposit will be sent to you in your pre-paid envelope as soon as inspections have been completed.

If you are leaving this summer but others are staying on, then you must clean and tidy your own room and ensure that the inventory for the house has been checked before you go.

If any tenants have already left the house when you receive this letter, would you please inform them of its contents.

Yours sincerely,

Ivor Castle.

----

i) Final Account

----

101 Rachman Ave.
Cooltown,
CL12 7GG

Dear *Wanda*,

RE: Your tenancy at .... - Final Account

Following your recent departure from the property, I have now completed my inspection and I am writing to give details of any deductions from your deposit.

The deposit held is £

The deductions to be made are as follows:

1. In communal areas (shared between all tenants):

Removal of rubbish
General cleaning
Cleaning of cooker
Defrosting and cleaning of fridge/freezer
Repairs to furniture
Repairs to house and decoration
Expenses incurred in liaising with utilities, rental companies etc
For contractors' bills or other communal charges

Replacement of missing items:

Total deduction (divided by no. tenants): £   **(a)**

2. In your own room (charges against you personally)

Cleaning
Repairs to furniture
Repairs to walls and decoration
For keys not returned (or replaced during tenancy)

149

Replacement of items missing from your room:

Other charges:

Total deduction: £ **(b)**

3. For rent or bills (charges against you personally):

For unpaid rent/ bills

For interest charged on those occasions when your rent was overdue without prior agreement

For 'bouncing' cheques
For charges I incurred in collecting late rent from you

Total deduction: £ **(c)**

Total deductions (a + b + c): £

Balance of deposit remaining after deductions: £

Yours sincerely,

Ivor Castle.

Appendix B

Documents for the Notice Board

a) Inventory

Property: 1 Campus View, Cooltown, CL1 6PR

INVENTORY OF FURNITURE AND FITTINGS, June 2006

Please check this inventory as soon as you move in. All electrical apparatus has been checked and is working safely. At the end of the contract period, charges *may* be made for items missing or damaged. Each tenant is provided with a room key, a window key where needed, and keys to external doors. These should be returned at the end of the tenancy.

UPSTAIRS

Front bedroom

Double bed	Mirror
Desk	Bin
Chair	Curtains
Two chests of drawers	Carpet
Side table	Light shade

Middle bedroom

Double bed	Chair
Wardrobe	Mirror
Locker	Bin
Chest of drawers	Curtains
Desk	Carpet

Back bedroom

Double bed	Bookcase
Wardrobe	Bin
Chest of drawers	Curtains
Desk	Carpet
Chair	Light shade

En-suite shower room
Mirror
Loo brush

Landing
Two light shades
Carpet

DOWNSTAIRS

Front bedroom

Double bed	Square table
Desk	Two shelves
Chair	Bin
Chest of drawers	Curtains
Bed settee	Carpet
Bookcase	Light shade
Mirror	Wardrobe

Hall
Two light shades

Hall cupboard
Vacuum cleaner
Broom
Mop and bucket
Dustpan and brush
Ironing board

Middle bedroom

Double bed	Cabinet
Chest of drawers	Mirror
Chair	Bin
Desk	Curtains
Wardrobe	Carpet

Sitting room
Two settees
TV table
Notice board
Carpet
Light shade

Kitchen

Fridge-freezer
Cooker
Grill pan
Roasting tin
Swingbin
Fire blanket
Three trays
Three oven dishes
10 bowls
Measuring jug
10 glasses
10 mugs
Three egg cups
Teapot
10 knives
10 forks

10 teaspoons
10 dessert spoons
Two cutlery trays
2 chopping boards
Scissors
Cake knife
Tin opener
Corkscrew
Three graters
Two fish slices
Whisk
Serving spoon
2 draining spoons
Masher
Two peelers

7 kitchen knives
Wooden spatula
Two frying pans
Colander
Egg poacher
Four saucepans
10 side plates
10 dinner plates
Condiment set
Butter dish
Cake tin
Kettle
Measuring jug
Garlic crusher
Draining rack

Bathroom

Cupboard
Mirror
Loo brush
Shower curtain
Bin

----

b) Bathroom ventilation

BATHROOM VENTILATION

Please ensure that the ventilator fan in the bathroom is left permanently switched on. The fan is fitted with a humidistat that activates the fan whenever the air moisture level rises (e.g. when someone is showering) and it switches off automatically when moisture levels reduce. This minimises condensation levels and restricts the growth of black mould.

It also helps if the window is opened as frequently as possible.

Many thanks,

Ivor

----

c) Council Tax

COUNCIL TAX

In order for me to claim council tax exemption on your behalf I need a photocopy of your enrolment form/council tax letter, which certifies that you are engaged in full-time study. Failure to provide the Council with this document *could* result in a tenant having to pay Council Tax.

Would you therefore please place your document in the envelope provided and I will collect it on Wednesday 4th October.

Many thanks,

Ivor

----

d) Fire

FIRE PROCEDURE

The procedure in the case of fire is:

EVACUATE THE PROPERTY

DIAL 999 TO CALL THE FIRE BRIGADE

DO NOT RETURN UNTIL ADVISED THAT IT IS SAFE

EMERGENCY CONTACT DETAILS

To contact the landlord in an emergency:

Call: 07967 555555

For repairs, contact the landlord. If the landlord cannot be contacted, but ONLY if the situation is URGENT, the following approved contractors should be called out:

Gas appliances:	Raj the Plumber 07944 555555
Electrical:	Sparky the Electrician 07930 555555
All other repairs:	Tom the Builder 07933 555555

----

e) From the Landlord

The document below is emailed to all my new tenants after they have signed tenancy agreements and I also post it on notice boards. It answers most questions before they are asked.

☺ GETTING THE MOST FROM YOUR TENANCY ☺

I've prepared some notes below that I hope are helpful, whether or not you've already lived in a shared house. If you've got any questions, give me a ring or drop me an e-mail.

Getting on with your landlord!

In all my dealings with tenants I try to be cheerful, polite, friendly, efficient and responsive. I want you to be happy with your tenancy and to get good value for the money you pay me. In return, I expect the same sort of approach from you: that you will read your tenancy agreement carefully and try to meet its obligations; that you will treat me with respect and courtesy; and that you will want us to have a friendly, non-adversarial relationship.

Very occasionally (and it is rare!) I come across tenants who never return my calls or messages and whose method of reporting problems in the house is to be confrontational and rude, in the belief that landlords only respond when shouted at or threatened.

The opposite is actually the truth. I will always go out of my way to help people who treat me with kindness and consideration. I feel less inclined to help those who are rude and unappreciative – they end up getting a minimal level of service, and feel the full force of penalties if they breach their tenancy agreement in any way.

Rent deadlines ☠ ☹

I know, it's something you'd rather not think about, but I must mention the subject! In the past, one or two tenants have given me the impression that they thought paying rent was optional, and that the deadlines were set entirely arbitrarily!

The deal is that I provide you with an essential roof over your head in exchange for you providing me with essential income! So, please ensure that your rent payments reach me **by** the dates on your tenancy agreement. I'm prepared to accept post-dated cheques from people who contact me first to discuss it.

If you wish to pay in cash, please don't post it! Ring me to arrange safe delivery.

Please note, you are supposed to send or deliver the rent to me, not me to come to you! If I have to come to you, or have to keep sending you messages, I may end up charging you for it!

I understand and acknowledge that almost all students have very limited financial means – I was one myself and had to work my way through university without a grant or a loan – and I will always try to be as sympathetic as possible. But that does not mean I am running a charity!

If your rent is late I will try to contact you first. The worst thing you can do is to avoid me! It puts pressure on you and frustrates me. I've always found that even 'impossible situations' can usually be resolved by talking. If you still don't respond, I will contact your rent guarantor. Persistent late-payers may have charges imposed, as described in the tenancy agreement.

The absolute bottom line is that you could be evicted if you don't pay your rent, and then I could take you and/or your guarantor to court to recover the unpaid rent and all my costs.

This is something I would do only when all communication has broken down, and as a very last resort. But the consequences for the tenant don't end there because having a County Court judgment against you means that you would be unable to get credit – loans, overdrafts, mortgages, etc. in the future.

I'm sorry if that all sounds heavy but it's important that everyone understands their obligations from the start, so that there are no tears at the end! If you ever need to discuss something with me on a confidential one-to-one basis, just give me a call. You can come to see me privately if it helps. ☺☺☺

Council Tax ✦❋ ☹

If you think landlords are a problem, try getting on the wrong side of the local council!

The rules about who should pay Council Tax are illogical, to say the least. Provided everyone in the house can prove they are full-time students there is nothing to pay. But if only one person is a part-time student (who, in my experience, are usually the poorest students of all!) then 75% of the Council Tax is payable. If two or more are part-time students, then 100% is payable.

I will claim exemption on your behalf. All you need to do is to provide me with a photocopy of your enrolment form or letter from the university that shows you are a full-time student. I will collect these from you all in early October. **BUT,** if you don't provide the document, the Council will send a bill....

Cleaning and maintenance ✦☹

Cleaning

OK, so if you want to live like a pig for a whole year and never clean your room or change your sheets (it's been known), then that's your choice.

But when it comes to kitchens, bathrooms and sitting rooms, hey, come on guys! Things work best when you put up a rota and spit-roast anyone who falls out of line.

So, agree who should clean the loo, empty the bins, wash the floors etc so that the communal areas are safe and hygienic. Alternatively, some tenants in the past invited their mums for the weekend....☺☺ But just bear in mind that most rows in student houses are caused by one person expecting everyone else to clean up!

Oh, and please DO use a sheet to cover your mattress (even if you don't change it often!). Soiled mattresses are expensive to replace! Please do not call me out to fix your vacuum cleaner until you've checked that the bag is empty and that the pipes, roller etc are not bunged up with hair, fluff and other bits. Vacuum cleaners do not like picking up coins, bottle tops, hair grips or pieces of paper larger than a few square centimetres so, if someone in your house has tried this, most likely the vacuum cleaner is blocked.

Maintenance

I take a lot of pride in my properties and try to keep them in tip-top condition. During the summer months a LOT of cleaning and maintenance takes place, and I have a regular team of contractors who are on call throughout the year.

I need your help to maintain standards, so please look after the house you are renting, and don't hesitate to call me if there is a problem. It doesn't follow that you will be charged for the repair.

Your house has been re-wired and has a safe, modern fuse board. Find out where it is located *__before you are plunged into darkness!__*

Fuses will trip out if you overload the system or if you use faulty appliances. Sometimes they trip if a light bulb blows. Check which switch has tripped and try turning it on again. Usually, that does the trick. If it won't stay on, give me a call, and I'll suggest further action. If you can't reach me, and it's urgent, call **Sparky the Electrician 07930 555555**.

If the pilot light on your boiler goes out, check that the power is on and then try re-lighting it according to the instructions. Again, if you get stuck, give me a call. If you can't get me, call **Raj the Plumber 07944 555555.**

You are responsible for keeping the small drains clear of rubbish and unblocking them, but if you get a sewer blockage or sewage overflowing from a manhole, call me immediately.

If you can't reach me, call Mid West Water on 0800 784 211. If the blockage is not their responsibility they will recommend a contractor to do the job but please don't call a contractor unless you have made every effort to contact me first, because they are VERY expensive.

For any other building emergency – plumbing, repairs etc call **Tom the Builder 07933 555555**, but only if you can't get me first!

I REPEAT, PLEASE DON'T CALL OUT ANY OF THESE GUYS UNLESS IT IS AN EMERGENCY AND UNTIL YOU HAVE TRIED ME FIRST, OTHERWISE YOU MAY END UP PAYING THEIR BILLS.

I **really** don't mind being called out to fix things (yes, this is a landlord speaking!) but here are a few call-outs from recent years that may make you think twice before dialling!

> *'Can you come and see to the knob in my bedroom?'*
> *'Can you take down my net curtains cos it's too private.'*
> *'Someone has urinated on my ceiling from the room above.'*
> *'Can you fix the toilet cos the room moves round when I sit on it'*
> *'The freezer door won't shut cos there's too much ice inside.'*
> *'My bed broke when my boyfriend jumped off the wardrobe.'*
> *'I think the electricity is leaking.'*
> *'Can you come and do something about the cellar cos it's scary.'*
> *'The broom won't sweep. Am I supposed to push or pull it?'*
> *'The bed broke when we all got out.'*

Usually I will come and do a repair (or send one of the guys) free of charge. But I might ask you to pay if your misuse or negligence has caused the repair. So, don't forget to defrost freezers occasionally, to de-scale kettles and showerheads, and to keep outside drains free of leaves.... oh, and empty the vacuum cleaner!

But if something needs fixing, please don't delay in calling me out – some breakages get more serious if they're not attended to straight away. Unless it's urgent though, try not to call me out of normal office hours – I've got a life too!

If I send a contractor, I'll usually give him keys so that he can get in if you are all out. All my contractors have been with me a long time and are very reliable and trustworthy. All repairs will be done quickly as possible – really!

Smoking ☹☹

Smoking legal substances is OK provided everyone in the house has agreed when and where it is permissible.

For obvious reasons it's not a good idea to smoke beneath a smoke alarm and if you smoke very heavily in a room that is painted white or cream, the fumes will discolour the walls and ceiling and you may be charged for a re-paint. (Use of incense has the same effect, and same consequences!)

Infestations ☹☹

In any house there are always other non-paying tenants who, but for your cleanliness and vigilance, will want to take over the place.

These squatters are often unseen, but can become a nuisance. We're talking insects and other vermin. Rest assured that a clean, well-ordered house will never have a problem, but if you leave uneaten food around overnight, or fail to put the bin bags into the dustbin, you're just inviting trouble.

Ants: they invade during the summer months and can be dealt with by spray or powder from a hardware shop. The spray works best because it creates a barrier over which they cannot crawl. Spray it around skirting boards and doorways once every few weeks, and you'll never have ants.

Slugs: these also come in summer and creep out at night, leaving silver trails over carpets (which rub off easily with your foot!). Follow the trail back to their point of entry (usually under a door) and put a few grains of coffee down. They won't come back.

Wasps: Wasps usually build nests under eves during June or July. The best thing is to shut the nearest window to stop them entering the house. DON'T try to tackle the nest yourself. If the wasps become a real nuisance, call the local council and they will recommend someone to deal with it, but there will be a charge. The wasps usually go of their own accord by late August.

Mice: I've never yet had a case of mice in a house but there's always a first time. If you find the corners of food packets have been chewed and see tiny dark pellets on shelves, then you've got a mouse. Either set a trap or put down poison.

Rats: I've read that the rat population in the UK now equals the human population, so you're never far from a rat. If you happen to see one rat scampering through the garden, don't panic, it may be en route elsewhere. But if you see one or several, more than twice, you may have an infestation.

If so, please call me immediately and I will come to inspect and, if necessary, get the council to send out a rodent officer. There is no charge for this.

Decorating your own room 🐀 ☹

Most likely your room is painted white or magnolia. The reason for that is because it's very easy to match the colour when touching up over marks and scratches at the end of the year. If you're into lots of deep purple with orange stars, then put up as many drapes and posters as you like, but please, **don't paint the walls.**

Leaving the property empty ✈ ☼

Break-ins rarely occur and where they do, it's usually young teenagers who make a mess, grab a few things they can carry, and run for it.

Although a determined burglar will get into any house, regardless of locks and security, it pays to deter them by making things difficult so:

- *never go out in warm weather without checking that you've shut and locked the windows*

- *if you are on the ground floor, draw your curtains so that anyone outside cannot see your computer, hi-fi, or other desirables*

- *always lock your bedroom door*

- *always lock the deadlock, not just the Yale, on your external doors. Where they are fitted, use the bolts on your back door.*

- *check that the security lights are working during darkness – they are triggered by movement within the sensor range – and call me if they are not.*

If you all go away for a period of more than just a weekend, e.g. Christmas, you need to take a few more precautions:

- *switch off all lights and close all internal doors. If defrosting the fridge/freezer, please make sure it's fully defrosted before you go, and leave the door open if it is turned off (or you'll come back to a crop of mushrooms!).*

- *DON'T turn off the central heating in winter – turn it down to come on for two bursts of about an hour each day – e.g. 02h00-03h00 and 14h00-15h00. This should be enough to protect against burst pipes (and the subsequent damage).*

- *DON'T leave behind any valuables that would be attractive to thieves e.g. electrical items. If you tell me when you are going, I'll try to pop round on a regular basis to keep an eye on things.* ☺

Ending your tenancy ✋

After Easter I will write confirming arrangements for the end of your tenancy and the repayment of your deposit. The letter will give guidance on how to prepare the property for handing back, and list examples of deductions that may be made from the deposit if things aren't up to scratch.

I always send out a final account showing the exact nature of any deduction. The main reasons for deductions include late payment of rent, lack of final cleaning, missing keys or other items, and so on. Most people adhere to the guidance and get all their deposit back. ☺

✉ Keep in touch ☎

If your contact details change, e.g. your mobile number or email address, could you please let me know? You never know when I might need you!

Send any updates to my e-mail address: *ivorcastle@topdigs4u.co.uk*

or by txt to **07967 555555**. Thx.

Have a great time in the house.

Ivor ☺

Advertising

a) Leaflet distributed in halls of residence.

WANT A HOUSE NEXT YEAR?

THEN SWITCH TO TOPDIGS! WE HAVE THE LARGEST STOCK OF
STUDENT HOUSES IN THE CITY.

All our properties are top quality and are situated in popular areas
on the west of Cooltown centre, close to the university main site or
the Alderman Gravytrain Site.

ALL ROOMS HAVE DOUBLE BEDS ☺

Houses/flats for student groups of 3 - 6

The quality of provision in all properties *meets and exceeds*
standards set by the university in its property accreditation scheme.

Features common to all properties include:

- Dry and well-ventilated
- Full compliance with safety legislation
  (Includes fire doors, smoke alarms, fire blankets,
  gas and electrical checks, safety locks etc)
- High standards of decor and cleanliness; gardening
  done free
- No water rates to pay
- Fully furnished
- Plumbing for automatic washing machines
- Cable and telephone lines to the property
- Central heating and double glazing
- Sitting rooms in all properties
- Security lighting

Visit our website for full details: **www.topdigs4u.co.uk**
For a viewing appointment text or ring: **07967 555555**

b) Recommended Website

Go to www.topdigs4u.co.uk to see a sample student landlord website.

The sample website has five main pages: the homepage, 'accommodation', 'safety info', 'testimonials', 'contact us'.

Each page should be topped and tailed with clickable links to all other sections.

Home Page

The homepage of the website should contain a brief introduction to you, the landlord and your properties. For example:

TOPDIGS PROPERTIES

Topdigs Properties is the leading private provider of student accommodation in Cooltown.

Established in 1986, we are a family business and do not use letting agents. This means that we maintain direct contact with our tenants and, as all members of our family are ex-university students, we know from first-hand experience exactly what students expect from their accommodation.

All of our properties are within easy walking distance of the university. All are warm, safe, dry and well ventilated. They are all fully furnished and equipped, have a good supply of electrical sockets and most study bedrooms have double beds. Most importantly, all rooms are cheaper to rent than the rooms provided by the university in its halls of residence.

Each property is completely refurbished when purchased, including re-wiring. Our safety standards exceed the minimum required by the housing authority or by the university accreditation scheme and we are fully responsive to any new legislation affecting rental property. Inspections are welcomed.

Rest of page: more photos of properties, landmarks and happy, smiling students.

Accommodation Page

The 'accommodation' page should contain an interactive city map showing the location of your properties. This enables the viewer to click on the property in question to obtain further details. Each property should have its own page.

Each of these will contain a photo of the property and details of its accommodation. It might look like this:

<u>Property 1: Five-bedroom house in Campus View</u>

PROPERTY DETAILS:
Five bedroom house, Campus View CL1.　　　　　[PHOTO HERE]

LOCATION:
0.5 miles from the city centre. 10-minute walk to Uni main site. Good public transport connection.

ACCOMMODATION:
Sitting room, kitchen, bathroom with shower, four large double bedrooms and one single bedroom, central heating, full double glazing, plumbing for washer, fully furnished. All-electric central heating.

RENT INCLUDES:
Water rates, servicing.

CONTRACT:
Assured short-hold tenancy, minimum 40 weeks (Sept-June). Returnable deposit and summer retainer. Summer contracts available. Rent payable termly or monthly. Discounts for contract renewal.

SUITABLE FOR:
Under/post grads sharing.

Safety Info Page

The 'safety info' page should contain details of all health and safety features in the properties, and references to relevant legislation or accreditation. This might include the following:

ALL TOPDIGS ACCOMMODATION IS FULLY COMPLIANT WITH SAFETY LEGISLATION AND EXCEEDS STANDARDS SET BY THE UNIVERSITY IN ITS PROPERTY ACCREDITATION SCHEME:

- All gas appliances checked annually.
- Periodic tests on electrical installations.
- Adequate supply of sockets.
- Mains-operated smoke alarms and heat sensors.
- Fire blankets in kitchens.
- Fire doors on kitchens, and all rooms in larger properties.
- Fire alarms and emergency lighting where advised.
- Thumb-turn locks on all doors.
- All soft furnishings 'fire proof'.
- Security lights and burglar alarms where advised.
- Regular health and safety inspections.

FEATURES COMMON TO ALL PROPERTIES INCLUDE:

- They are dry and well ventilated
- Full compliance with safety legislation
- High standards of decor and cleanliness
- Fully furnished
- Plumbing for automatic washing machines
- Cable and telephone installed
- Central heating and double glazing
- Double beds in most rooms

A TYPICAL STUDY BEDROOM INCLUDES:

Curtains, carpet, bed, desk, chair, bookshelves, wardrobe, chest of drawers, locker, easy chair, four to six electric sockets.

A TYPICAL KITCHEN INCLUDES:

Cooker, fridge-freezer, ample storage, crockery, cutlery, cooking utensils, saucepans, cleaning materials, vacuum cleaner, washing machine plumbing, six to eight electric sockets.

Testimonial Page

The last page should contain testimonials from your previous tenants (add lots of photos of smiling students around the quotes). For example:

"I would like to say how much we enjoyed living in such a nice student house in a friendly neighbourhood, and also how much we appreciated having such an organised and amenable landlord."
Hannah Fish, Wiltshire, 1995

"My daughter was a bit dubious about renting a house because of all the horror stories, but now, after two years in one of your houses, she has nothing but praise for you. Thanks a lot. It certainly put our minds at rest."
Pat and Alan Denby, Yorkshire, 1998

"I am writing to thank you for the excellent service you provided in renting the house to my friends and myself. You always dealt with our problems promptly and without hassle, for which I thank you kindly. I will take with me every fond memories of my time in the house."
Adam Crumpet, Suffolk, 2001

"We really enjoyed our stay in the house, and thanks again for renting it to us. I will recommend your name to anyone I hear that is going over."
Stephanie Colleen, Ireland, 2002

"Thank you very much, it was a pleasure living there."
Camilla Hurst, Aylesby Park, Lincs, 2003

Contact the Author

Tony Bayliss is available for consultancy, advice on business development, and to contribute to training events.

His e-mail address is freetrip@hotmail.co.uk. He says his 'intellectual property' can be rented at very reasonable terms!

Pay Less Tax!

...with help from Taxcafe's unique tax guides and software

All products available online at **www.taxcafe.co.uk/books**

How to Avoid Property Tax
By Carl Bayley BSc ACA

How to Avoid Property Tax is widely regarded as *the* tax bible for property investors. This unique and bestselling guide is jam packed with ideas that will save you thousands in income tax and capital gains tax.

"A valuable guide to the tax issues facing buy-to-let investors" - *THE INDEPENDENT*

Using a Property Company to Save Tax
By Carl Bayley

Currently a 'hot topic' for the serious property investor, this guide shows how you can boost your after-tax returns by 40% by setting up your own property company and explains ALL the tax consequences of property company ownership.

"An excellent tax resource....informative and clearly written" **The Letting Update Journal**

Tax-Free Property Investments
By Nick Braun PhD

This guide shows you how to double your investment returns using a variety of powerful tax shelters. You'll discover how to buy property at a 40% discount, paid for by the taxman, never pay tax on your property profits again and invest tax free in overseas property.

Property Capital Gains Tax Calculator
By Carl Bayley

This powerful piece of software will calculate in seconds the capital gains tax payable when you sell a property and help you cut the tax bill. It provides tax planning tips based on your personal circumstances and a concise summary and detailed breakdown of all calculations.

Non-Resident & Offshore Tax Planning
By Lee Hadnum LLB ACA CTA

By becoming non-resident or moving your assets offshore it is possible to cut your tax bill to zero. This guide explains what you have to do and all the traps to avoid. Also contains detailed info on using offshore trusts and companies.

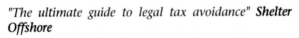

"The ultimate guide to legal tax avoidance" **Shelter Offshore**

The World's Best Tax Havens
By Lee Hadnum

This book provides a fascinating insight into the glamorous world of tax havens and how you can use them to cut your taxes to zero and safeguard your financial freedom.

How to Avoid Inheritance Tax
By Carl Bayley

Making sure you adequately plan for inheritance tax could save you literally hundreds of thousands of pounds. *How to Avoid Inheritance Tax* is a unique guide which will tell you all you need to know about sheltering your family's money from the taxman. This guide is essential reading for parents, grandparents and adult children.

"Useful source of IHT information" **What Investment Magazine**

Using a Company to Save Tax
By Lee Hadnum

By running your business through a limited company you stand to save tens of thousands of pounds in tax and national insurance every year. This tax guide tells you everything you need to know about the tax benefits of incorporation.

Salary versus Dividends
By Carl Bayley

This unique guide is essential reading for anyone running their business as a limited company. After reading it, you will know the most tax efficient way in which to extract funds from your company, and save thousands in tax!

Selling Your Business
By Lee Hadnum

This guide tells you everything you need to know about paying less tax and maximizing your profits when you sell your business. It is essential reading for anyone selling a company or sole trader business.

How to Avoid Tax on Stock Market Profits
By Lee Hadnum

This tax guide can only be described as THE definitive tax-saving resource for stock market investors and traders.

Anyone who owns shares, unit trusts, ISAs, corporate bonds or other financial assets should read it as it contains a huge amount of unique tax planning information.

How to Profit from Off-Plan Property
By Alyssa and David Savage

This property investment guide tells you everything you need to know about investing in off-plan and new-build property. It contains a fascinating insight into how you can make big money from off-plan property... and avoid all the pitfalls along the way.

How to Profit from Student Property
By Tony Bayliss

Tony Bayliss is one of the UK's most successful student property investors. In *How to Profit from Student Property* he reveals all his secrets – how he picks the best and most profitable student properties; how he markets his properties (ensuring they are rented out months in advance), and how he enjoys capital growth of 12% pa, year in year out.

Disclaimer

1. Please note that this guide is intended as general guidance only for individual readers and does NOT constitute financial, investment, accountancy, tax, legal or other professional advice. Taxcafe UK Limited accepts no responsibility or liability for loss which may arise from reliance on information contained in this guide.

2. Please note that the law and practices by government and regulatory authorities are constantly changing. We therefore recommend that for investment, accountancy, tax, or other professional advice, you consult a suitably qualified solicitor, accountant, tax specialist, independent financial adviser, or other professional adviser. Please also note that your personal circumstances may vary from the general examples given in this guide and your professional adviser will be able to give specific advice based on your personal circumstances.

3. Please note that Taxcafe UK Limited has relied wholly on the expertise of the author in the preparation of the content of this tax guide. The author is not an employee of Taxcafe UK Limited but has been selected by Taxcafe UK Limited using reasonable care and skill to write the content of this guide.